EX LIBRIS

SOUTH ORANGE
PUBLIC LIBRARY

WITHDRAWN

THE HOLOCAUST

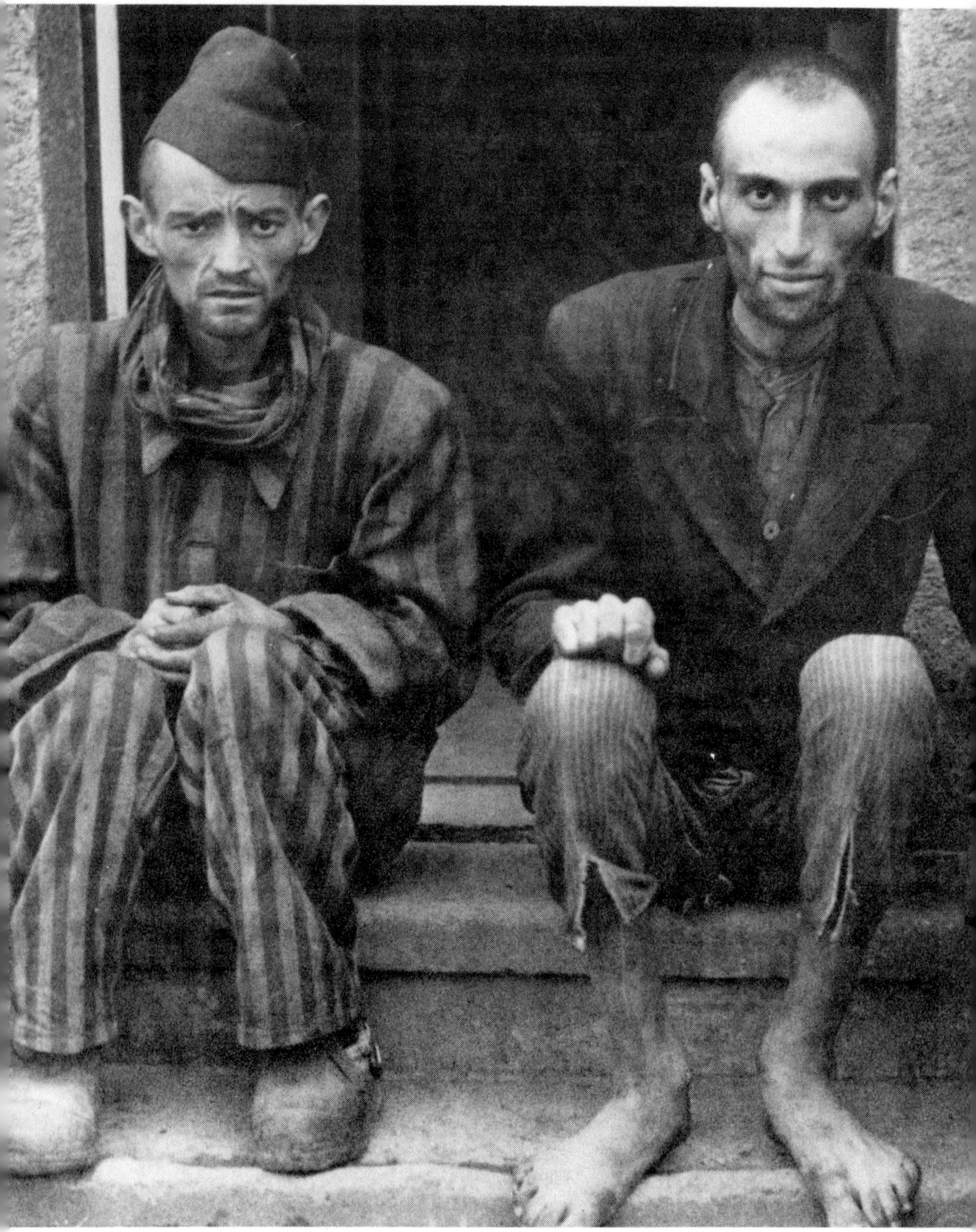

THE HOLOCAUST

THE FIRE THAT RAGED

BY SEYMOUR ROSSEL

Franklin Watts
New York / London / Toronto / Sydney / 1989
A Venture Book

Frontis: *two survivors of the Nazi concentration camp at Nordhausen, Germany, following their liberation by the Allied forces*

Library of Congress Cataloging in Publication Data

Rossel, Seymour.
 The Holocaust : the fire that raged / by Seymour Rossel.
   p.   cm. — (Venture)
   Bibliography: p.
   Includes index.
 Summary: Discusses the historical background, from the Treaty of Versailles through Hitler's rise to power, that led to the horrible and systematic slaughter of millions of Jews by the Nazis during World War II.
   ISBN 0-531-10674-8
   1. Holocaust, Jewish (1939–1945)—Juvenile literature.
   [1. Holocaust, Jewish (1939–1945)] I. Title.
              D804.3.R67   1989
 940.53'15'03924—dc19   88-26718 CIP AC

Copyright © 1989 by Seymour Rossel
All rights reserved
Printed in the United States of America
5 4 3 2 1

*For
David and Linda Altshuler,
involved with others,
they need never ask
for whom the bell tolls.*

Maps by Joe LeMonnier

Photographs courtesy of:
UPI/Bettmann Newsphotos: pp. 2, 21, 27 (top), 29, 34 (bottom), 37, 40, 67, 73, 76, 83, 100 (bottom), 105, 109; New York Public Library Picture Collection: pp. 15, 86; Archives of the YIVO Institute for Jewish Research: pp. 27 (bottom), 34 (top), 57, 62; Hoover Institution Archives, UNIO, Original Photograph in Envelope DJ, World War II Pictorial Collection: p. 44; Wide World/AP Photos: pp. 53, 80, 92; U.S. Army Photo: p. 100 (top)

CONTENTS

Chapter One
The Man Called Hitler
11

Chapter Two
The Nazi Party
24

Chapter Three
Laws, Riots, and War
32

Chapter Four
Hitler's Victories
42

Chapter Five
The Other War
50

Chapter Six
The Ghettos
56

Chapter Seven
The Concentration and Death Camps
65

Chapter Eight
Escape and Rescue
79

Chapter Nine
Revolt and Freedom
89

Chapter Ten
The End
97

Chapter Eleven
What Does It Mean to Be Human?
107

A Chronology of the Holocaust 113

For Further Reading 117

Sources Consulted 119

Index 121

THE HOLOCAUST

THE MAN CALLED HITLER

THE TREATY OF VERSAILLES

World War I lasted four years, from 1914 to 1918. The Allies—led by the United States, France, Great Britain, and Russia—defeated the Central Powers led by the German nation. At the end of the war, the Allies wrote a peace treaty and forced the Central Powers to sign it. It was called the Treaty of Versailles since it was signed in Versailles, France, in 1919.

The Treaty of Versailles was harsh, perhaps even unfair. It stated that Germany was guilty of having started the war. It took away one tenth of all of the land of the German Empire. It forbade Germany from raising a large army or building large weapons. And it said that Germany had to pay the Allies enormous sums of money to make up for the costs of the war.

The new German government was forced to sign this treaty. The German people felt betrayed. How could they put their faith in a government that would sign such a

EUROPE 1914

- Capitals
- Major cities
- Central powers

0 — 1000 Miles

EUROPE 1919

- Capitals
- ○ Major cities

0   1000 Miles

shameful treaty? The German people believed that the Allies had started the war, so the treaty hurt their pride. They were proud of their army and its strength, and now their army was weak. The war had made them poor, and giving money to the Allies meant new taxes that would make them poorer still. The new government was even weaker than the army, and many small political parties sprang up to attack it. In the end, instead of bringing peace, the Treaty of Versailles led to a second world war—a war more terrible than anyone could have imagined.

ADOLF HITLER

Adolf Hitler was born on April 20, 1889, in the village of Braunau am Inn in Austria. His father, Alois, was a customs official. Alois was very strict with his son and often beat him. Hitler seems never to have loved his father. Klara, his mother, was very religious and very protective of Adolf, who was an only child.

By the time he was twenty, he had lost both of his parents, had dropped out of school, and was living on an orphan's pension in Vienna. When he could find no work there, he moved to Munich, Germany. In 1914, he joined the German army. He was wounded twice during the war and received the Iron Cross, First and Second Class. Yet he never rose above the rank of corporal because his senior officers felt that he was a poor leader.

In the same year that the Versailles Treaty was signed, Hitler joined a small political group in Munich called the German Workers' party. The group met to discuss the weak German government and to complain about how much better things were before the war. They felt that the greatest dan-

Hitler (right) as a soldier during World War I with a comrade from his regiment

ger to Germany came from the Bolshevik Communists who had recently come to power in Russia.

Hitler soon became one of the seven leaders of the group. He wanted to do more than hold discussions. He wanted to create a force to change things. So he wrote out invitations by hand, asking people to come and hear him speak. When the evening of the speech arrived, however, only the seven party leaders were there.

Hitler was not discouraged; he tried again. He sent out mimeographed invitations for another evening, and this time eleven people came to listen to him. At last he decided that people were not really worried about the Bolsheviks. He needed to find something to talk about—a villain or a threat—that would really interest people and stir them up.

ANTI-SEMITISM

Reviewing German history, Hitler discovered a subject that the church had used for hundreds of years to stir people up—the Jews. For centuries, the church taught Christians to blame the Jews for the death of Jesus, even though the New Testament says that it was the Romans who put Jesus to death.

In the Middle Ages the Jews were persecuted in Germany just as they were in most of Christian Europe. They were forced to work as small traders and moneylenders (professions that were considered "sinful" by the Catholic Church). And they were often accused of cheating Christians in business and banking. In addition, whenever there was trouble in Europe—a plague, an unsolved murder, a polluted well—local priests would blame the Jews for causing it.

Using the Jews as a scapegoat—a group that could be blamed for any problem—is called *anti-Semitism*. Adolf Hitler believed that he could use anti-Semitism as a tool to help him become more popular. With the last of the party's money, he put an announcement in a local newspaper promising an evening of anti-Semitic speeches. This time a crowd appeared to listen.

At the meeting Hitler discovered something important. He was supposed to talk for only twenty minutes; instead he spoke for half an hour. The crowd was electrified, the applause immense. Hitler excited them. He discovered that he was a great speaker.

He spoke again and again. The party membership grew. In 1920 the party name was changed to the National Socialist German Workers' party—the *Nazi* party, for short. In the election of 1928, the Nazi party won 800,000 votes.

THE "BEER HALL *PUTSCH*"

Hitler used the money from new members to turn the Nazi party into something more than just another political group. He trained men to be "storm troopers," a kind of private army. And many important Germans, remembering the days when the German army was so glorious, began to support the Nazi party and its "troops."

Hitler grew bolder. Why wait to be voted into power? Why not use the troops to seize power just as the Bolsheviks had done in Russia? On November 8, 1923, Hitler and his storm troopers surrounded a group of government officials in a beer hall in Munich and told them that they had to swear loyalty to his "revolution" or else he would destroy them.

The government officials swore loyalty to Hitler, but as soon as they were free, they turned on him and had him arrested. He was tried and given the lightest possible sentence, five years in prison with a possibility of parole after only six months. His "beer hall *Putsch*" had failed, but news of it spread, and Hitler's name was heard far and wide for the first time.

MEIN KAMPF

Hitler served nine months before he was pardoned. In jail, he made friends with another prisoner, Rudolf Hess, who offered to put Hitler's ideas into a book. Hitler spoke, and Hess put what he said on paper. The book was called *Mein Kampf* ("My Struggle"), and from the moment it was printed it became the Nazi bible. In *Mein Kampf*, Hitler set forth his main ideas:[1]

Anti-Semitism • Like most extremists, Hitler was full of prejudices. The most passionate prejudice of all was reserved for the Jewish people. From beginning to end in *Mein Kampf*, Hitler blamed the Jewish people for all of the troubles and ills that Germany was suffering.

Racism • Hitler said that the Jews were the natural enemies of the "superior" Aryan race (the Northern European group to which most Germans belonged). Hitler be-

---

[1] Adolf Hitler, *Mein Kampf* (New York: Houghton Mifflin, 1943).

lieved that it was wrong for Aryans to marry Semites (Jews) and have children. He said that the Aryan race should remain "pure" and was afraid that Jewish blood would "poison" the pure blood of the Aryan Germans, weakening the Aryan race. This notion that human beings can be powerful only if they remain racially pure was an important idea in *Mein Kampf.*

Lebensraum • Hitler not only claimed that the Aryans were a "superior" race but also that they deserved a greater share of the land of Europe. He reminded the Germans that the Allies had taken away a part of Germany after World War I. He said that their idea was to keep the Germans from having *Lebensraum*—"space for living." The Aryans would grow strong again only when they had seized more *Lebensraum* for their race.

The "Jewish Plot" • Hitler also argued that Jews were dangerous because they had virtually taken control of the German nation. The Jews, he said, controlled the government, the land, the banks, and the press. This last was especially dangerous, he said, because the Jews used the press to tell Germans what they should think. In *Mein Kampf,* Hitler called this "the Jewish plot."

THE GREAT DEPRESSION

Freed from prison, Hitler returned to the work of building his party and its troopers. World events helped. In the fall of 1929, in the far-off city of New York, the Wall Street stock market crashed, and the Great Depression began. Millionaires who had put their money into stocks became paupers overnight. Banks that had put their money into stocks closed their doors. People in the middle class who had their money in banks or in stocks suddenly found that they had no money. Companies went bankrupt; factories and stores closed. Jobs were scarce.

Germany had borrowed enormous sums of money from U.S. banks. Suddenly the Germans found themselves even worse off than before. To pay their debts and taxes, people in Germany were forced to sell their houses and furnishings. The Depression was like the straw that broke the camel's back. Coming on top of the German defeat in World War I, the shameful Treaty of Versailles, and the postwar years of inflation and unemployment, the Depression brought a feeling of utter hopelessness to the people of Germany.

The major political parties were stunned and helpless. Only two parties could turn and say, "We told you so." One of these was the Communist party. The other was the Nazi party.

HITLER'S PATH TO POWER

Hitler crisscrossed the country by plane, by automobile, and by railroad. He made as many as three speeches a day. He blamed the loss of World War I on the old German government. He told the people that they had been betrayed by Jewish bankers and moneylenders. He said the time had come to rebuild the German army and to prepare for war against the Communists in Russia. He promised there would be jobs for everyone when the Nazis came to power. Earlier he had spoken to hundreds of people at a time; now thousands came to listen to him.

Hitler (standing, far right) and other leaders of the Nazi party celebrating their victory after the 1930 election. They are giving the Fascist salute.

In the elections of 1930, the Nazi party won 6.5 million votes. They were the second largest political party in Germany. They now owned more than a hundred seats in the *Reichstag,* Germany's congress. Military and business leaders began to take Hitler seriously. They knew that new factories and industries would be needed to build a stronger army. The middle class took him seriously, too. They knew that new factories and new industries would mean more jobs for them.

Hitler dressed his storm troopers in brown uniforms and called them the Brownshirts. By the mid-1930s they were an army of nearly half a million men. By 1933, most small anti-Semitic parties had joined forces with the Nazis. The aging president of the German republic could not find a moderate leader to form a new government. Finally, on January 30, 1933, the president called on Adolf Hitler to be the new chancellor of Germany. Hitler swore the oath of office, promising to protect the German constitution and its laws and to be just and fair to all Germans.

THE *REICHSTAG* FIRE

Even as he spoke these words, Hitler was making plans for a war on German democracy. New elections were set for March 1933, and Hitler wanted to be certain that the Nazis would win decisively. Most historians agree that it was Hitler and his storm troopers who planned and set the fire that broke out in the *Reichstag* building in 1933, but, of course, Hitler blamed the fire on the Communists.

Before the fire, Hitler and his chief followers made a list of the people they would arrest. The list included many of the leading members of the *Reichstag,* leading members of the German Communist party, and many leaders who had spoken out against Hitler and the Nazi party. Arriving at the scene of the fire, Hitler swore to arrest everyone "responsible." Instead, he set about arresting all of the people on his list.

The quick arrest of so many of Germany's foremost politicians left their parties with no leaders. The government seemed about to collapse. Hitler said that the Communists were trying to take over Germany by force as they had done in Russia in 1917. He persuaded the German president to sign an emergency decree "for the protection of the people and the state."

HITLER BECOMES DICTATOR OF GERMANY

The decree canceled all individual and civil rights. It placed all power in the hands of Hitler and his party. It made it illegal for Germans to express their beliefs freely, to assemble to hear political speeches (except Hitler's, of course), or to come together in large groups for any other reason. The decree also made it legal for Hitler to control what was said in newspapers or on the radio. The Nazis were now free to open and read mail, to read telegrams, to listen in on telephone conversations, to search houses without warning, and to confiscate personal belongings.

In fact, shortly after the presidential decree of February 28, 1933, Adolf Hitler became the absolute dictator of Germany. He could say and do just about anything he pleased. No king had ever been more powerful.

THE NAZI PARTY

As the spring of 1933 approached, Germany was a dictatorship with Hitler as the supreme power. True, new elections were coming, but most of the country's leaders were in prison, and no party but Hitler's was allowed to make political speeches or to hold political gatherings. Everywhere, people were frightened. Money was scarce. Food was scarce. Jobs were difficult to find. And people truly believed what the press wrote—that the Communists of Germany were trying to take over. In all of Germany, only Hitler's Nazi party seemed to promise that things could get better.

Despite this, most Germans did not like Hitler. The Nazi party managed to win less than 50 percent of the national vote. Hitler was forced to include some moderate leaders in his new government. In another time and place, this might have kept him from totally controlling Germany.

While Hitler was making speeches and forming the government, the Brownshirts looted, wrecked, and burned the offices of the Communist and Socialist parties. They arrested and attacked additional political leaders. They destroyed the Socialist newspapers in many states.

One day before the newly elected *Reichstag* met, Heinrich Himmler, one of Hitler's key assistants, proudly announced that the first "concentration camp" had been built in Dachau, not far from Munich. In this camp, he said, the many arrested Communist and Socialist leaders would be "concentrated" and held so that they could no longer be "dangerous" to Germany.

By July of 1933, Hitler was able to say, "the [Nazi] party has now become the [German] State." All other political parties were outlawed. No new parties could be formed. Only the Nazi party remained.

WHO JOINED THE NAZI PARTY?

Hitler's Nazi party was more than just a political group. It was an army, too. Hitler called his Brownshirts by their "official" name, the *Sturmabteilung,* or *SA.* Especially at first, they were an army of criminals. Most of the Brownshirts had been in prison at one time or another. Hitler also organized his own secret police force, the *Gestapo,* and his own personal bodyguards, the *Schutzstaffel,* or *SS* (nicknamed the Blackshirts). Later the *SS* took charge of all security for the German state.

Most people who joined the Nazi party were just average citizens of Germany who looked forward to the day when Hitler would make good on his promises. They were people who wanted jobs, who needed food, who were scared by Communism, who believed what the church had taught them about the Jews being evil, and who believed that

Hitler would be an effective leader. Many were unable to read or think for themselves and were fooled by Hitler's powerful speeches. Many others were impressed by his popularity among the Nazis. Nearly all of them closed their eyes to the evil that Hitler and his party were doing and put their blind trust in the new dictator.

Some were guilty of more than just following the wrong leader. Some German leaders helped Hitler because they thought it would bring them money or success. Many of the young officers supported Hitler because he said he would rebuild the army and strengthen it. Many business leaders, professors, church leaders, scientists, and others jumped on the bandwagon because Hitler's popularity was on the rise. These were people who were well educated and who should have known better. They should have spoken out against the evils that Hitler perpetrated.

There was one other group of party members that Hitler was especially interested in—young people. During his rise to power, Hitler made youth movements an important part of his plan. He and his followers organized young people into the so-called Hitler Youth, teaching them that Nazism was the best hope for the future. Later, when Hitler became dictator, he made sure that the same lesson was taught in every public school. He even had textbooks rewritten to say that Jews were the cause of Germany's

Above: *stormtroopers, also known as Brownshirts, march by Adolf Hitler standing in the car at left.*
Below: *Hitler Youth marching.*

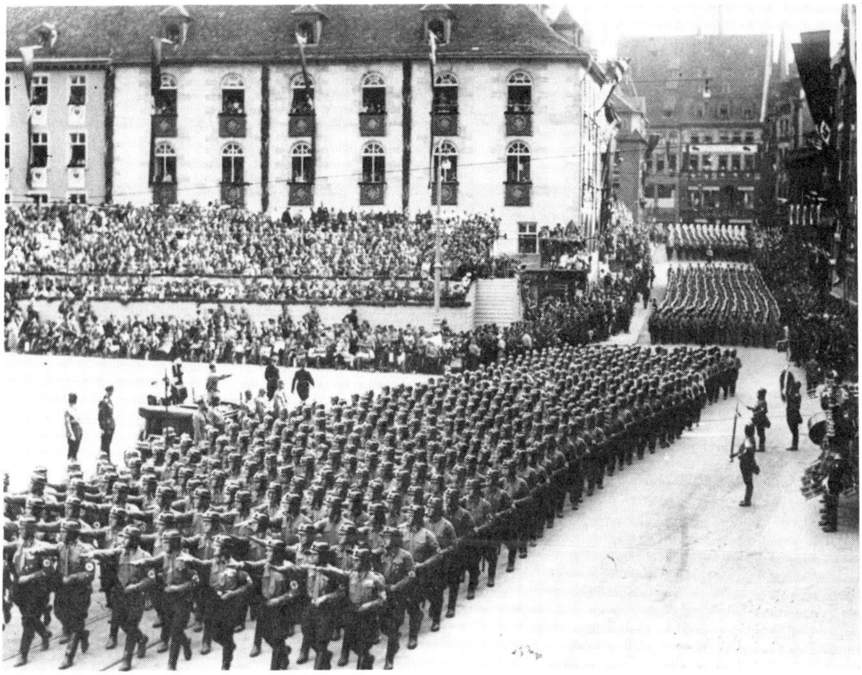

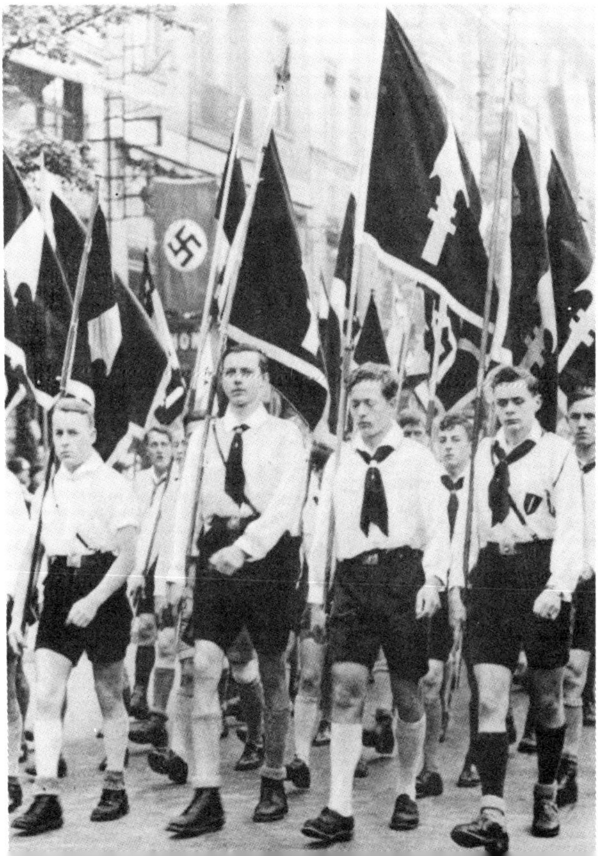

problems, that all Communists were either Jews or followers of Jews, and that only the Nazis could protect Germany. As young people graduated from school and from the Hitler Youth movement, they went into the army. In this way, the army grew more and more helpful to Hitler.

THE USE OF PROPAGANDA

Hitler was a master of propaganda, the spreading of lies and half-truths to promote a cause. His party even had an official "minister of propaganda," a man named Joseph Goebbels. Just as he used propaganda in the schools and in the Hitler Youth to teach his beliefs, Hitler used it to convince the German people that he was the answer to their many needs.

As dictator, he was in control of everything that was written in newspapers and spoken on radio (there was no television broadcasting yet). Newspaper reporters and radio newscasters soon learned that they would be fired or sent to prison if they did not please the government with what they said or wrote. Nearly everything that Goebbels sent to them they repeated as the truth, whether or not it was.

People heard what Hitler wanted them to hear. They read what Hitler wanted them to read. In the end, most of them believed what Hitler wanted them to believe.

Official propaganda told the German people that they were the greatest race on earth—pure Aryans, large-boned, strong-muscled men and women with blond hair and blue eyes. (Hitler taught this, even though he, himself, was short and dark.) Official propaganda told them that they were "superior" and the Jews were "inferior." Official

Minister of Propaganda Joseph Goebbels studies a speech before a broadcast to the German people.

propaganda told them that the Jewish people were their enemies. Slowly but surely, most Germans came to believe what they were told. Hitler proved that propaganda was indeed a mighty tool.

Meanwhile, Hitler continued to speak to huge crowds, repeating the same lies over and over again. He and his followers taught the German people to salute him by raising one arm. His speeches continued to excite the people; his popularity grew with each passing day. And hatred of the Jewish people grew at an alarming rate.

THE JEWISH SCAPEGOAT

Hitler chose the Jewish people as his special scapegoat for several reasons. First, there was his personal prejudice against the Jews. Second, out of jealousy and ignorance, there were many who, like Hitler, were already prejudiced against the Jews. More to the point, the church for many centuries had singled out the Jewish people as a scapegoat. Through the centuries, the Jews had been accused of almost any evil that caused suffering to their Christian neighbors.

Jews first came to Germany in the early days of the Christian era as traders following Roman armies. They stayed and were joined by more Jews. Over the years, the Jewish community grew larger and larger. Nearly 100,000 Jews served in the German army during World War I (nearly 12,000 were killed fighting for Germany). By the late 1920s, there were more than a half million Jews in Germany, and more than 150,000 lived in the capital city of Berlin.

RACISM AND SCIENCE: AN UNHOLY MARRIAGE

To the church's anti-Jewish teachings, Hitler and his followers added a new dimension—racism. Racists believe that people inherit certain qualities from their race, or human group. In *Mein Kampf,* Hitler spoke of the good qualities of the Aryan race and of the bad qualities of the Jewish "race." (Actually, Jews are not a separate race; they come from a human group called Semites that includes Jews, Arabs, and several other peoples.) Hitler promoted the idea that Jews were naturally wicked and inferior.

Most scientists, doctors, lawyers, artists, and educators found the idea of racism ridiculous, but Hitler found enough people to agree with him. They spent their time and efforts trying to prove that different races of people had different kinds of blood. (Today we know that all people everywhere share the same blood types.) They tried to show that inferior blood could make a person criminal or cruel or unintelligent. (Today we know that blood types do not influence any of these qualities.) Those scientists and educators who agreed with Hitler were given the best jobs and the highest salaries. In the end, it even became dangerous for a German to speak out against the idea of racism.

Textbooks used in schools and colleges were changed to say that Jews were inferior. Students were forced to study what was called "German" science, "German" mathematics, "German" chemistry, and "German" physics. Even fairy tales were rewritten to say that all devils and evil villains were Jews.

• • •

Hitler and his followers had found a pathway to power. They learned that the thoughts of the German people could be controlled through the use of propaganda. They discovered that the hearts of the German people could be united in hatred against a common enemy, the Jews. By the spring of 1933, they were ready to put these two tools to work to create a new kind of modern nation—one founded on prejudice and willing to destroy anyone or anything that stood in its way.

LAWS, RIOTS, AND WAR

USING LAW AND ORDER

The new dictator of Germany, Adolf Hitler, decided to use the law to change Germany into a Nazi state. On April 1, 1933, he ordered that no German should buy anything from a Jewish merchant or store for that day. Then he waited and watched to see what would happen. The German people obeyed willingly; almost none of them entered a Jewish shop that day.

Bolder now, on April 7 Hitler ordered all non-Aryans to stop working for the government. Thousands of Jews who worked in local, state, or federal offices lost their jobs. On April 21, Jews were forbidden to slaughter animals or prepare meat according to Jewish law. On April 25, it was announced that fewer Jews would be admitted to German universities.

Some Jews decided to leave Germany. They were forced to leave behind everything they owned—their savings, their belongings, whatever they had. But most Jews believed that things could not get any worse. They stayed in the hope that the anti-Semitic fever would soon cool. But the fever had just begun; before it would be over, it would become a madness.

THE NUREMBERG LAWS: 1935–1938

From 1933 to 1935, there was a short period of quiet for the Jews. Hitler was busy shaping and strengthening his government. In August 1934, the aged president of Germany died, and Hitler declared himself chancellor and *der Führer* ("Leader") of the German people for life. No one opposed him; democracy was entirely defeated. Hitler and the Nazis grew stronger. By the fall of 1935, Hitler was again ready to turn his attention to "the Jewish question."

On September 15, 1935, the *Reichstag* met in the city of Nuremberg to pass laws that were known afterward as the Nuremberg Laws. These laws stated that the Jews were now "subjects," with none of the rights of German citizens. Jews could not marry Germans or hire Germans to work in their homes. One year later, a law was passed forbidding Jews from voting in German elections.

Again, the German people showed that they were willing to let Hitler continue in his anti-Semitic campaign. In shops and lawyers' and doctors' offices, people put up signs saying, "Jews Not Welcome." Jewish workers lost jobs in many businesses and factories. And more Jews were put out of work in July 1938, when a law was passed saying that Jews could no longer be brokers, office man-

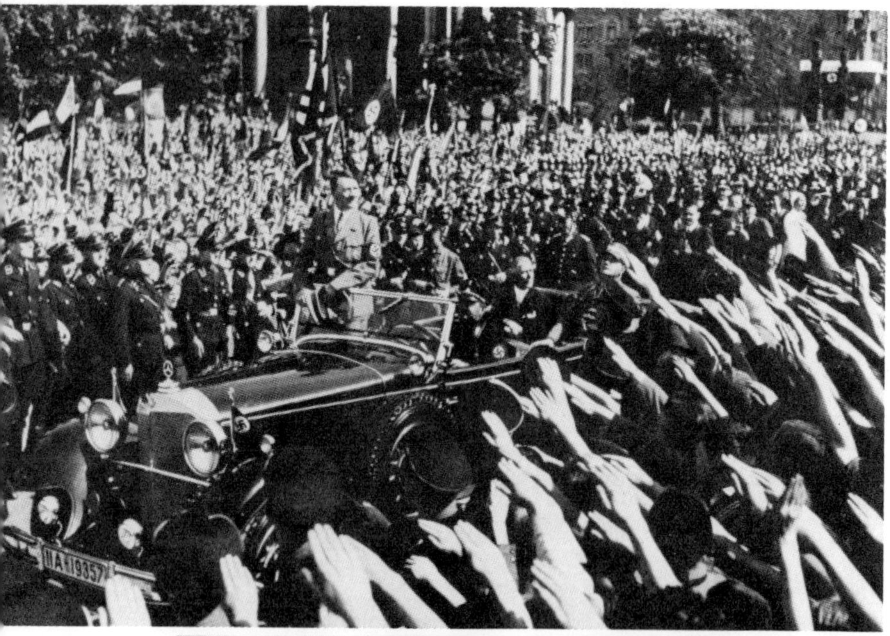
IIA-19357

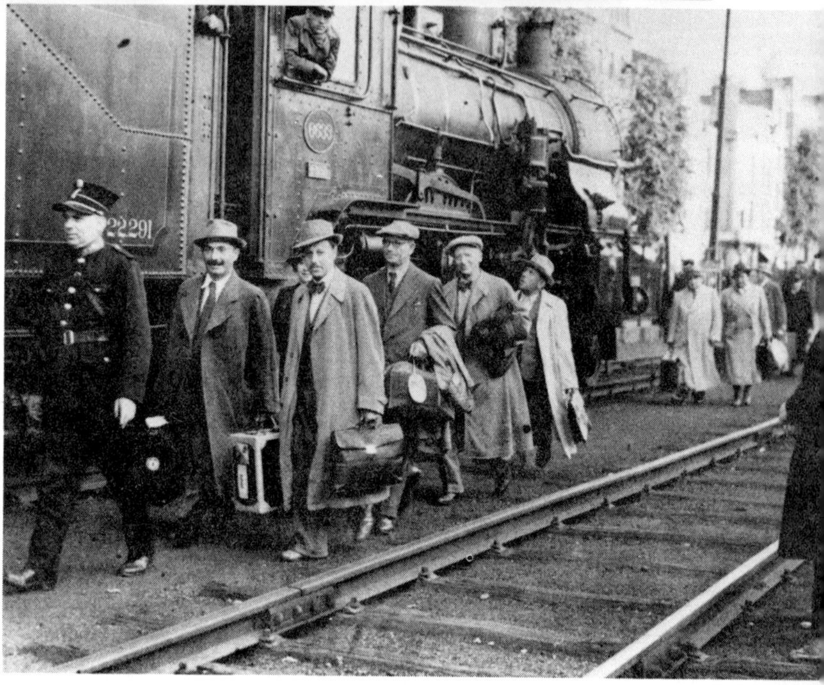
22291

agers, tourist guides, or real estate agents; in September 1938, a law was passed stating that Jewish doctors could be only "medical assistants" from then on.

The Nazis changed street names that sounded Jewish. They forced Jews whose first names did not sound "Jewish" enough to add "Israel" or "Sarah" to their names so that they would not be mistaken for Germans. They forced Jews to carry special identity cards and marked passports carried by Jews with a *J* for *Jude*—the German word for Jew.

THE FIRST DEPORTATION: OCTOBER 1938

The Nazis clearly wanted the Jews to leave Germany. Yet leaving was not easy. Many Jews were too poor to travel. Others had no place to go. The countries around Germany refused to allow poor Jews to enter, and Germany refused to allow the Jews to leave with any money. Hitler turned the problem over to one of his chief followers, Reinhard Heydrich.

Heydrich knew that many of Germany's poorest Jews were really Polish citizens. In October 1938, he and his

Above: *Der Führer being enthusiastically greeted by a large crowd of Germans in May 1935.*
Below: *German Jewish refugees arriving in the Antwerp, Belgium, railroad station enroute to sanctuary in Holland.*

men rounded up nearly 15,000 Jews. The Nazis took all of their belongings from them and sent them by train to the German-Polish border. Then they pushed the Jews across the border into Poland. The Polish border guards were so startled that they began to fire their weapons at the approaching thousands. Finally, however, when the guards saw the Polish passports that the Jews were carrying, the gates were lifted; and men, women, and children—most of whom had not eaten for two days—poured into Poland.

One of the Jews wrote to tell his son in Paris about the terrible border crossing. His son was so angry that he decided to take revenge on the Nazis. On November 7, he put a gun in his pocket and went to the German embassy in Paris. In the hallway of the embassy, he drew his pistol and killed a minor German official. The assassin was arrested by the German guards and taken away, never to be seen again. But what he had done signaled the beginning of an endless nightmare for the Jews of Germany.

NOVEMBER 9–10, 1938: "THE NIGHT OF BROKEN GLASS"

On the day that the German official in Paris died, Propaganda Minister Goebbels demanded that the people of Germany take revenge against the Jews. Heydrich sent instructions to local police everywhere not to interfere. He even sent instructions to Nazi police to take part in "demonstrations" against the Jews. The rioting began on the evening of November 9 and continued for two days. The riots were called *Kristallnacht*, "the Night of [Broken] Glass."

Germans gaze upon a Jewish-owned shop destroyed in Berlin during Kristallnacht. The broken glass symbolized the anti-Semitism Hitler had fostered in Germany during the 1920s and 1930s.

Synagogues were burned, and stores were looted and destroyed. Germans broke into Jewish apartments, stealing belongings and smashing what they did not steal. Heydrich ordered the arrest of as many Jews as local prisons could hold, especially, he added, "rich Jews." Many of the arrested were sent to concentration camps, some never to be seen again. For two days, Jews were thrown out of moving trains and buses, beaten up, and humiliated. Many of those who tried to escape were shot.

In all, 191 synagogues were burned, 76 more totally destroyed. Cemetery chapels and community centers were torn down. Thousands of businesses were ruined. Large stores were ransacked. Over 20,000 Jews were arrested, and 72 were killed or seriously wounded on the spot. As fires burned, the fire brigades stood and watched. The German police stood and watched as Germans stole Jewish property. Sometimes, the police even joined in the looting.

When it was all over, the Nazis discovered that they had a new problem. Most Jewish homes and businesses were covered for losses by German insurance companies. For broken windows alone, the claims came to 6 million marks—an enormous sum! Hermann Goering, the Nazi in charge of Germany's economy, complained to Heydrich, "You should have killed two hundred Jews and done less property damage."[2] To save the economy, Goering ordered that the Jews, not the insurance companies, should pay the damages!

---

[2] Nuremberg Trial Document PS 1816.

New laws forbade Jews to own businesses and to attend plays, movies, concerts, or exhibitions. Jewish children were expelled from public schools, and special curfews were set up for all Jews. Jews had to ride in the back of buses or trains. They were not allowed out on the streets on Nazi holidays. They were forced to sell property and to hand over stocks, bonds, and jewelry to the government.

THE WAR BEGINS

In the meantime, Hitler was making plans for war. Just as he had promised, new factories and industries were turning out weapons and supplies to build a new army. In March 1936, Hitler marched his troops into the Rhineland, a strip of land on both sides of the Rhine River that had been off-limits to Germans since World War I. No government tried to stop him. In March and April of 1938, he sent his troops into Austria. In March 1939, he sent his troops into Czechoslovakia. The rest of the world watched, hoping with each new conquest that Hitler would be satisfied. Hitler, however, continued to speak of needing *Lebensraum,* "living space," for the Germans; and he turned his eyes toward Poland.

Hitler gathered his army along the German-Polish border. He knew that his armies were not yet ready to fight both Russia and Poland at the same time. So even though he hated the Russians, he entered into a treaty with them. Both countries promised not to attack each other.

On September 1, 1939, Hitler sent tanks and troops into Poland, as the German air force attacked from the

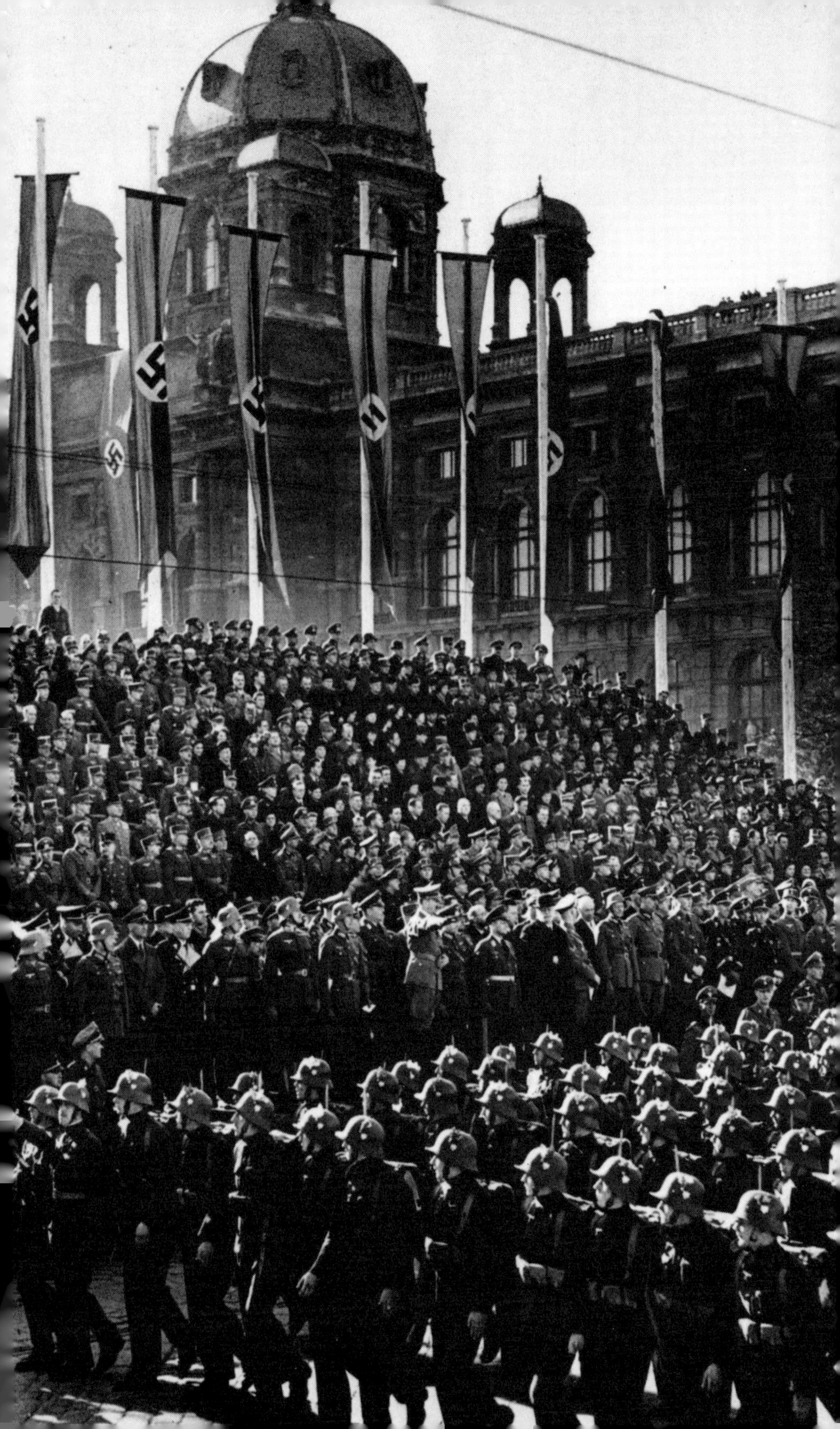

sky. The Poles fought against tanks and airplanes with foot soldiers and men on horseback. They were defeated in only five days. This rapid and devastating style of military warfare came to be called the *Blitzkrieg,* or "lightning war."

On September 3, 1939, Britain and France declared war on Germany. World War II had begun.

Hitler salutes his troops during their victory parade in Vienna.

HITLER'S VICTORIES

CHOOSING SIDES

France and Germany were ill-prepared for a real war, but the battle lines were drawn. Britain and France—later joined by Russia—were called the Allied powers. Three dictatorships joined together to form the Axis powers—Germany, Italy, and Spain. Later, they were joined by Japan.

In the weeks after the conquest of Poland, Hitler was pleased to see that the Allies were not preparing to attack his western borders. For one thing, many pieces of German equipment had been damaged in Poland. For another, most of his troops were still in Poland, far away from the German border in the west. Germany might have been defeated if the Allies had attacked in those early weeks. To Hitler's relief, they did not.

Instead, Russia attacked and conquered a country friendly to Germany, Finland. In their treaty, the Russians had only promised not to attack Germany. But, using the excuse of declared war, Russia saw the chance to win Finland and seized it while the German army was still in Poland. Hitler was angry. He was frightened that Russia and the Allies might next attack Norway and Denmark and come at him from the north.

To keep this from happening, Hitler marched his troops into Norway and Denmark, saying that he wanted to "protect" them. Throughout the war, he kept troops in these countries, but both of them proved thorns in his side. Time and again, small groups of Norwegians banded together to attack Germans inside Norway or to do battle against German ships in Norwegian waters. Denmark often refused to carry out Hitler's anti-Jewish programs and resisted every German attempt to expel Danish Jews.

HITLER INVADES HOLLAND AND BELGIUM

Hitler now had to make a major decision. He wanted to attack Russia to destroy his old enemy, the Communists, but he was afraid that France and Britain might choose that moment to attack him from the west. He knew that his armies were not yet strong enough to fight in both the west and the east. At last he decided to turn his forces westward. On May 10, 1940, German armies marched into Belgium and Holland. Both countries fell to the Germans within days.

It was a clever plan. As Hitler had hoped, the armies of France and Britain marched toward Holland and Belgium, even as Hitler sent part of his army to the south toward France. In a matter of weeks, the French and British armies were caught in a trap between the Germans to the north, south, and east of them. Their backs were to

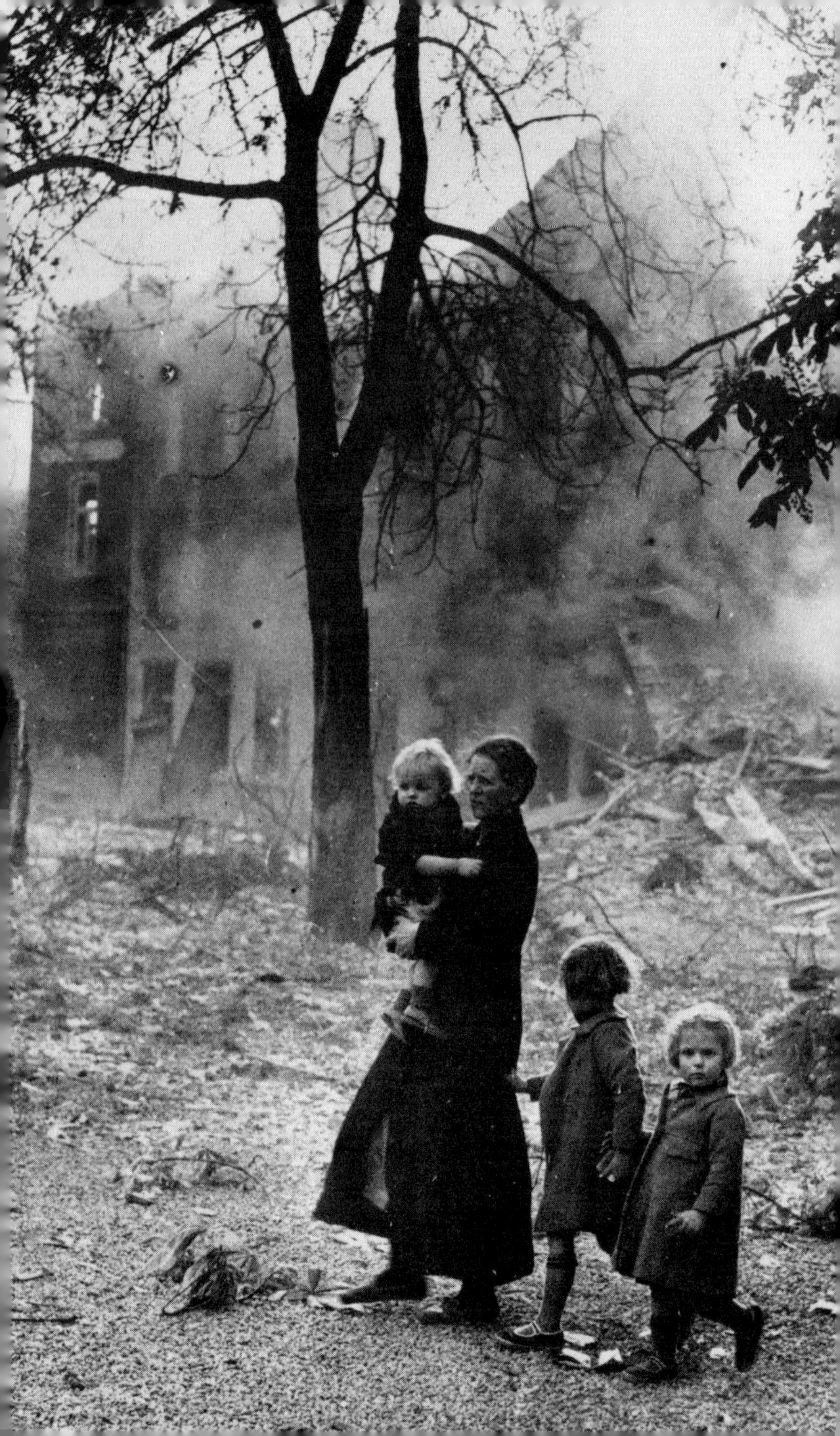

the sea, and four divisions of German tanks were closing in for the kill. The British and French armies seemed doomed.

Just then Hitler decided to alter his plan. He ordered the tanks to stop where they were and let the air force, the *Luftwaffe,* attack. But things did not go well. The British Royal Air Force bravely battled the *Luftwaffe* in the skies above Dunkirk, as more than 300,000 British, French, and Belgian soldiers were rescued by sea and taken across the English Channel to safety. The Allied armies were saved, but at a terrible cost.

FRANCE—HITLER'S GREATEST CONQUEST

On June 21, 1940, France surrendered to Germany. In Germany, Hitler was called the greatest military leader of modern times. He had defeated the French, sent the British running, and conquered most of Europe.

For a while, he thought of sending troops into Britain. But between Europe and Britain was the sea, and Britain still had the strongest navy in the world. So Hitler again turned his attention to Russia, more ready than ever to attack the hated "Communist Jews" there.

Hitler was all set to attack Russia when the Italians decided to attack Greece. As Hitler feared, the Italians

Belgian refugees walk amidst the destruction of war in that country.

EUROPE 1941

- Capitals
- Major cities

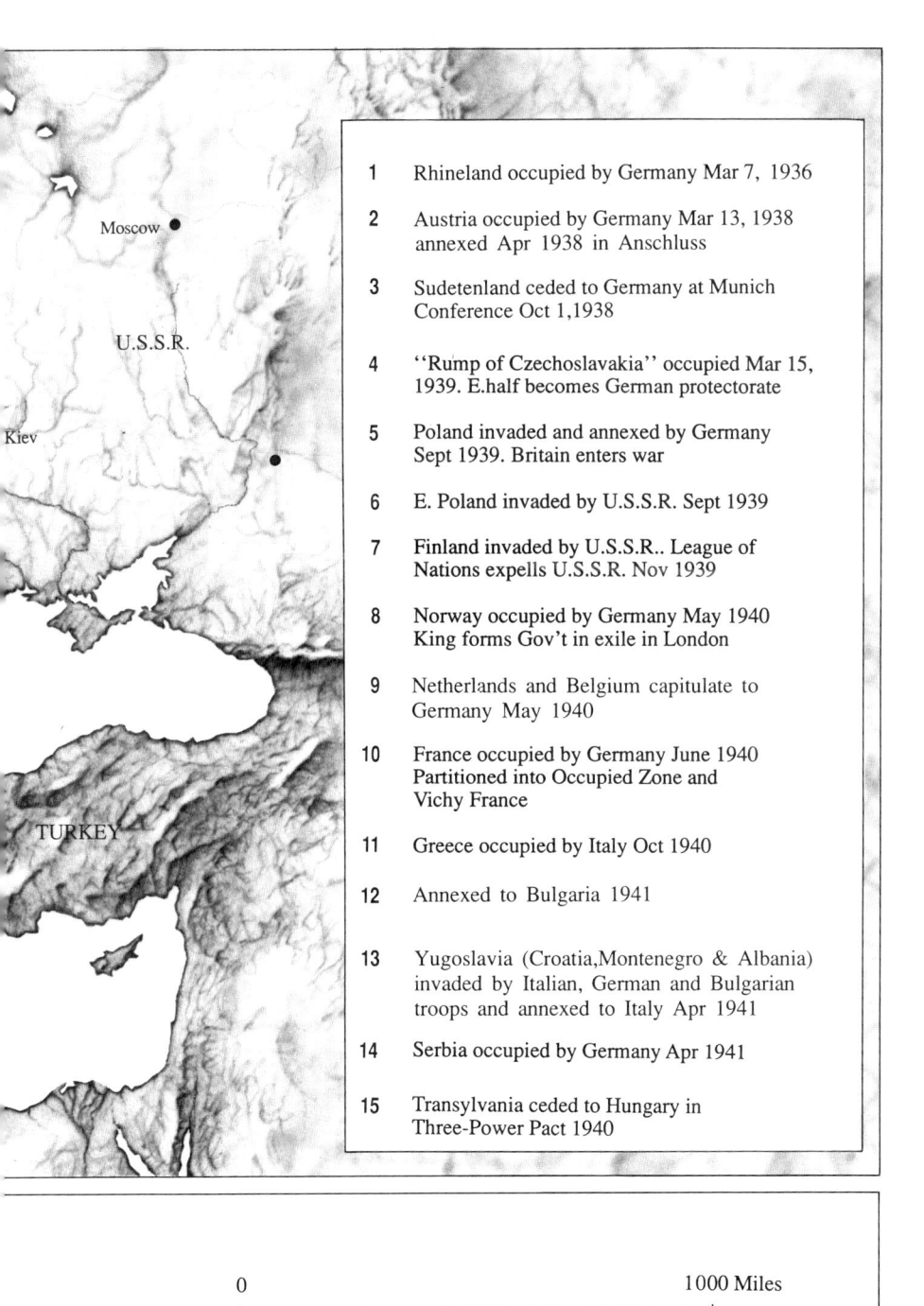

#	
1	Rhineland occupied by Germany Mar 7, 1936
2	Austria occupied by Germany Mar 13, 1938 annexed Apr 1938 in Anschluss
3	Sudetenland ceded to Germany at Munich Conference Oct 1,1938
4	"Rump of Czechoslavakia" occupied Mar 15, 1939. E.half becomes German protectorate
5	Poland invaded and annexed by Germany Sept 1939. Britain enters war
6	E. Poland invaded by U.S.S.R. Sept 1939
7	Finland invaded by U.S.S.R.. League of Nations expells U.S.S.R. Nov 1939
8	Norway occupied by Germany May 1940 King forms Gov't in exile in London
9	Netherlands and Belgium capitulate to Germany May 1940
10	France occupied by Germany June 1940 Partitioned into Occupied Zone and Vichy France
11	Greece occupied by Italy Oct 1940
12	Annexed to Bulgaria 1941
13	Yugoslavia (Croatia,Montenegro & Albania) invaded by Italian, German and Bulgarian troops and annexed to Italy Apr 1941
14	Serbia occupied by Germany Apr 1941
15	Transylvania ceded to Hungary in Three-Power Pact 1940

0   1000 Miles

were much too weak to conquer the fiercely resisting Greeks. Worried that the British might help Greece and attack Germany from the south, he was forced to help Italy by sending twenty-nine divisions against Greece. The war in Greece was over in only four weeks, but it was a month's delay that Hitler had not wanted.

He looked for help to fight Russia among the Axis Powers, but without success. Japan refused to attack Russia from the east, Spain refused to attack the British outpost at Gibraltar to keep the British busy, and Italy was too weak after its war in Greece to be of any use. In the end, Germany was forced to act alone in Europe.

THE ATTACK ON RUSSIA

On June 22, 1941, 3 million German soldiers, more than 7,000 cannon, and 3,500 tanks crossed the border into Russia. The Russian air force was quickly defeated by the *Luftwaffe*. Russian tank divisions were outrun and destroyed. The Russian army fought bravely, suffering one loss after another and slowly falling back toward Moscow, the Russian capital. The war in Russia dragged on. The precious summer months turned to fall; the fall turned to winter. It was October before the German army could see Moscow in the distance.

By December the weather was below zero, and the German army had still not conquered Moscow. Worse, they were still in their summer uniforms. The German *Blitzkrieg* had slowed to a hopeless creep. Behind them, the Russians had burned the crops so that the Germans would have to transport their food supplies from faraway Poland. Soldiers died of hunger and of exposure to the cold. Hitler knew that the armies had to be called back before they were utterly destroyed.

BAD NEWS FROM THE FAR EAST

Hitler had no luck at all with his Axis group. Just when his troops were growing desperate in Russia, the Japanese decided to go to war against the United States. On December 7, 1941, the Japanese bombed Pearl Harbor in a sneak attack. At once, the United States joined the Allied powers, declaring war on Japan and on Germany.

Hitler's hours of victory were over. Now began the long, slow years of defeat.

THE OTHER WAR

THE WAR AGAINST THE JEWS

As Hitler's armies overran country after country, the Jews of Europe were taken by surprise. In each country the Nazis conquered, they put their propaganda to work, spreading the lies of racism and anti-Semitism. They forced countries to pass laws like those in Germany, to isolate the Jews and separate them from the community. It was as if Hitler was taken in by his own propaganda. Even while he was directing the war against the Allies, he seemed to think that he was fighting another, equally important, war against the Jews.

GHETTO AND *SHTETL*: THE JEWISH QUARTERS

In the fourteenth century in Spain and Portugal, Jews were forced to live apart from non-Jews. In 1516, in Venice, Italy, the Catholic Church ordered that walls be built around the Jewish quarter. Venice called this walled-in quarter the *ghetto*, probably taking the name from that of a nearby ironworks. At night, the ghetto gates were locked, and guards were posted to make certain that the Jews would not come out until daybreak. In part, the Catholic Church wanted to protect the Jews from attack by superstitious peasants. But the church also wanted to separate Jews from Christians, which only led to more superstition among the peasants.

In a short time—and for similar reasons—ghettos appeared throughout Western Europe. Jews were sometimes forced to wear special badges on their clothing (another idea the Nazis would later borrow), and Jews were not allowed to own land or work in certain professions. In Eastern Europe there were few ghettos. Instead, Jews lived in small sections of towns called *shtetls*. There were no walls around the *shtetls*, but Jews were still separated from the non-Jewish community.

What the church—Catholic and Protestant—really wanted was to convert the Jews to Christianity. To do this, it tried to make Jewish life uncomfortable. Jewish holy books were burned. Jews were forced to sit through long sermons promising hell to those who died Jewish and heaven to those who converted. This was the great difference between the anti-Jewish behavior of the church and the anti-Semitic behavior of the Nazis. The church wanted to destroy Judaism by converting Jews; Hitler wished to destroy Judaism by destroying the Jews themselves.

THE GHETTOS DISAPPEAR

Jews lived in the ghettos until the end of the Middle Ages, right up to the time of Napoleon Bonaparte. Napoleon, however, decided that the Jews could be a help to him. As his armies conquered Europe, they tore down the ancient ghetto walls and set the Jews free. In this way, Napoleon gained the loyalty of the Jews of Europe. In time, these Jews told legends about the great Napoleon, making him into a folk hero.

When Napoleon was defeated, a few ghettos were rebuilt. For the most part, however, Jews were allowed to mix with non-Jews as they had never done before. Some countries, including Germany, even made the Jews full citizens. By the beginning of the twentieth century, German Jews often claimed that they were "Germans first, Jews second."

Germany's Jewish citizens became lawyers, physicians, businesspeople, writers, and professors. Though they were only 1 percent of the total population, the majority of Germany's leading scientists were Jewish, a great many of them winners of the Nobel Prize. Two of Germany's greatest composers were Jewish—Gustav Mahler and Arnold Schoenberg. And Heinrich Heine, the writer called "the Shakespeare of the German language," was also Jewish. In many ways, being Jewish in Germany before the time of Hitler was like being Jewish in America today.

SEPARATING THE JEWS

The Nazis changed all that. At first, they separated Jews from non-Jews in many small ways. In her diary, Anne Frank, a teenage Dutch Jew, tells how this worked:

> *Jews must wear a yellow star, Jews must hand in their bicycles, Jews are banned from trains and are forbidden to drive, Jews are only al-*

A Jewish couple walking along a street in Berlin wearing the six-pointed yellow star with the inscription Jude *(Jew) sewn on their clothes*

lowed to do their shopping between three and five o'clock and then only in shops which bear the placard "Jewish shop." Jews must be indoors by eight o'clock and cannot even sit in their own gardens after that hour. Jews are forbidden to visit theaters, cinemas, and other places of entertainment. Jews may not take part in public sports. Swimming pools, tennis courts, hockey fields, and other sports grounds are all prohibited to them. Jews may not visit Christians. Jews must go to Jewish schools. . . . So we could not do this and were forbidden to do that.[3]

THE MEDIEVAL GHETTO IN A NEW WAY

The Nazis borrowed the medieval idea of the ghetto and gave it new life in Poland. They gathered Jews from all quarters of the city and forced them to live together in a few square city blocks. They forced the Jews to build stone walls around the "Jewish quarter," leaving only one or two gates that could easily be guarded.

Before the Jews entered the ghetto, their belongings were taken from them. Calling this "Aryanization," the Nazis would then give the property to people of the Aryan race. In many cases, the property seized by the state was used only by the Nazis themselves. Once Jews were in the ghetto, they were put to work as slave laborers. They were forced to sew uniforms for the German army, to make

---

[3] Anne Frank, *The Diary of a Young Girl* (New York: Pocket Books, 1952), 63.

ammunition, to build roads, and so on. As long as they worked, they were fed. If they stopped working, they were given no food.

In September 1939, Heydrich issued an order saying that all Polish small-town and *shtetl* Jews had to be removed to the large cities, where the *Gestapo,* the Nazi secret police, could "watch over them." By 1941, most Polish Jews were in the slums of Warsaw, Kovno, Krakow, Lublin, and other cities. Western Jews, including those from Germany, were moved by train into Poland to join them.

As the war pressed on, the Jews were ignored or forgotten by most of the rest of the world. Hitler and the Nazis were free to do what they would with the Jews. And what they would do was almost beyond belief.

THE GHETTOS

We know a great deal about the kind of life that the Jewish people were forced to live in the ghettos. Many diaries, letters, and manuscripts were smuggled out, and many more were found after the war was over. A large number of these came from the ghetto in Warsaw, Poland. What they tell us about life in Warsaw was true of life in all of the ghettos.

THE WARSAW GHETTO

In Warsaw, almost half a million Jews were squeezed into a few city blocks in which only 145,000 people had lived before the war. There were 1,500 buildings there, with fourteen or more people forced to live together in each apartment. There were no gardens or open spaces, so finding fresh air or a place to be alone was nearly impossible. With so many people in such a small space, disease spread quickly, and there were many epidemics. In 1940 a typhus epidemic struck. The fever spread so quickly, and there

The Warsaw ghetto packed with people

was so little medicine, that within a few weeks nearly 16,000 Jewish lives were lost.

Sickness was a great danger to life, but an even greater danger was starvation. There was no food in the ghetto. The Jews had to depend on the Nazis to supply them with food. They were given no meat, fish, fresh vegetables, or fruit. Instead, they were given bread, potatoes, and fats to live on; and each person was given only enough to make up about 800 calories a day. (A full-grown man uses about 2,000 calories a day just to keep up his normal body weight.) People by the dozens died of starvation.

There were fifteen entrances to the Warsaw ghetto, each guarded by Polish and German soldiers who had orders to shoot on sight any Jew who even came close. Only Jews in work gangs, closely watched by *Gestapo* men, were allowed to leave the ghetto. Those workers, and small children who could sneak over the wall or through the sewers beneath the city, often smuggled food and firewood into the ghetto. Such smuggling was always risky. Those who were caught were immediately put to death, and, in the end, smuggling helped little, if at all.

GOVERNMENT IN THE GHETTO

The Germans had no offices in the ghetto and seldom appeared there. For a while, they amused themselves by conducting tours for German soldiers on leave, showing the soldiers how Jews were dying in the streets. But this upset many of the soldiers, so the tours were canceled in 1942.

To control the ghetto, the Nazis set up Jewish "councils," the *Judenräte*.

The Judenräte—To Cooperate or Not? • The people of the Judenräte had to obey German orders or they would be replaced. To enforce their decisions, the Nazis also set up Jewish "police forces." The Nazis gave them uniforms, armed them with whips and clubs, and allowed them to terrorize other Jews. Many of these Jews had been criminals before the war; others thought that this was a way of keeping themselves and their families alive. In the end, however, the Jewish police were sent to their deaths along with all of the other Jews.

In general, the *Judenräte* tried to watch over the sanitation and health of the people in the ghetto, running its clinics and hospitals. It was also in charge of assigning people to work forces, both inside and outside the ghetto. Jews in the ghetto often tried to bribe members of the *Judenräte* in exchange for favors—for example, assignment to special work forces, changes of apartment, or jobs on the Jewish police. Some members of the *Judenräte* found they could become rich and powerful by accepting these bribes. In fact, the council members or the council head sometimes found that, by cooperating with the Nazis, they could become like royalty in the ghetto.

Where the *Judenräte* accepted bribes or cooperated with the Nazis, things grew worse and worse for the Jews in the ghetto. On the other hand, where the *Judenräte* pretended to cooperate but really worked to help the Jews, more Jews survived and the ghettos caused more trouble for the Nazis.

The SS—Threats and Deception • The Nazi *SS* used threats against the Jews in the ghetto. Sometimes they threatened that if the *Judenräte* would not turn over a certain number of Jews, thousands of Jews in the ghetto would be killed. Using blackmail like this, they slowly emptied out one ghetto after another, sending the Jews to concentration camps.

Sometimes the Nazis just lied. For example, in Kovno in 1941, the Germans told the *Judenräte* that they needed 500 young scholars for a special task. They said that these scholars would not have to work at hard labor. The *Judenräte* drew up a list; young people even volunteered for this special duty. The scholars were chosen. They were never seen again.

"Transportation" to the East • The Nazis lied about something else; they said that those taken from the ghettos were being "transported" to work in the east. Sometimes postcards came from people who had been transported—one postcard, and never another. There was no return address.

The Jews began to realize that something terrible was happening. They heard rumors that the people being transported were being sent to concentration camps to be starved, or to death camps to be gassed. But most Jews in the ghettos found these rumors too incredible to believe.

The Roundups • Most Jews believed that the Nazis were sending them to the east to work at hard labor. That seemed bad enough. They began to resist when the Nazis came to transport them. Families struggled to stay together. Jews hid when they heard that the Nazis had entered the ghetto to conduct a "roundup." The Nazis threatened the members of the *Judenräte*. Any resistance, they said, would mean death for all of the Jews in the ghetto.

Those caught in a roundup were packed into overcrowded boxcars on trains. There was no extra space. They were forced to remain standing, sometimes for several days, as the train took them to the death camps. A few Jews were lucky enough to escape from these trains, but most could not.

WHY JEWS SELDOM FOUGHT BACK

In the ghettos, death came quickly for thousands—death from disease, death from the cold of the Polish winters, death from starvation. In the early years of the war, many people in the ghettos suffered and died, but revolts were rare. Why? There were many reasons.

Fear of Reprisals • One was the fear of reprisals—that the Nazis would take terrible revenge for any revolt. When a revolt did break out, the Nazis did not bother to look for those who caused it to punish them. Instead, they simply killed other Jews by the thousands. Thus, many of those who wished they could revolt did not, hoping to save others from dying needlessly.

Belief That it Would Soon End • Still others did not revolt because they were sure that the war could not last forever. When it was over, they believed, the Nazis and the people of Poland would again act like decent folk. In the meantime, they tried to find ways to "get along." Some bought from smugglers or became smugglers. Some kept on working, hoping that they would be useful to the Nazis and not be transported or killed.

Children in the Warsaw ghetto eating soup. Many children who lived on the streets were not so fortunate.

Need for Food • Others were simple country people who had been transported to the ghettos from *shtetls* and small towns. For them, the city was a confusing place, and the closed-in life was unbearable. Many of them had no homes. They slept in the streets and begged for food. Some even lost the will to live, suddenly giving up and dying of hunger, cold, disease, or a broken heart. Those who did not die had only one thought: to find food. For people who needed to spend every waking moment in the search for food, there was no time to think of rebellion.

The Jewish Police • Another reason that there were few revolts in the ghettos was the Jewish police. They were the only Jews allowed to carry weapons, and they were more interested in having power over other Jews than in fighting the Nazis. Fear of them kept many other Jews from fighting.

THE JEWISH WAY OF LIFE IN THE GHETTOS

The Nazis controlled the ghettos, but they could not control the feelings of the Jews. Inside the walls of the ghettos, the Jews created a way of life based on Jewish teachings. Even as their bodies starved, they tried to keep their spirits alive. Many of them continued to study and to write. Reading became more popular than ever before. The few books in the ghetto were read again and again, passed from one person to another, shared by everyone.

Sending Children to School • Schools in the ghetto were forbidden, but teachers continued to work. They held classes for children and for adults. Jews in the ghetto continued to prepare for an imagined future by studying Hebrew, English, mathematics, science, and many other things. Diplomas were given, and being a good student was still a mark of pride.

Maintaining Jewish Culture • Jewish actors formed theater groups to entertain the Jews in the ghetto. Jewish painters continued to paint with whatever they could find—crayons, chalk, even homemade paints. They held exhibits of their paintings. Historians kept on writing—often the history of the ghetto itself. Reporters kept interviewing people and writing columns for papers that did not exist. Those who had a little money went to the coffee houses at night to sip smuggled liquor or watered-down coffee. Those who had no money for the cafés gathered to tell jokes and share stories. Though death was everywhere, young people still found the courage to marry and even to have children.

THE MODEL GHETTO: THERESIENSTADT

In Czechoslovakia, the Germans set up a special ghetto at a place called Theresienstadt. They gave meat and vegetables to the people there and even made sure that there was enough living space for everyone. To this special ghetto they sent well-known Jews, decorated war veterans, and old people. Of course, when Jews were transported out of this ghetto, they were sent to their deaths, but the Nazis kept life at Theresienstadt bearable for a good reason: Like all criminals, they wanted to hide the truth of what they were doing from the rest of the world.

Whenever the International Red Cross demanded to inspect German ghettos or concentration camps, the Nazis took them only to Theresienstadt. Nothing terrible seemed to be happening there. And that is what the Red Cross reported. As far as most of the outside world was concerned, Jews in the ghettos were being treated decently.

THE CONCENTRATION AND DEATH CAMPS

Lord Acton, a British historian, once said that "power tends to corrupt, and absolute power corrupts absolutely."[4] In Hitler himself and in all the Nazis who were given power over the Jews, any sense that what they were doing was wrong was set aside in favor of their Nazi beliefs.

HITLER AND HIMMLER ORGANIZE THE *SD*

Hitler chose Heinrich Himmler to command the *SS* (which had once been Hitler's personal bodyguard). Himmler's assignment was to use the *SS* to destroy the Jews. For this task, Himmler used the security police, or *SD (Sicherheitsdienst)*, a branch of the *SS*. And Himmler hand-picked Reinhard Heydrich to be in charge of the "Jewish ques-

---

[4] Lord Acton (John Emerich Edward Dalberg-Acton), letter to Bishop Mandell Creighton, April 5, 1887.

tion." Since the *SD* operated mainly within the borders of Germany, Heydrich also worked with the *Gestapo* police to control the Jews in lands that Hitler had conquered.

It was Heydrich who discovered *SS* major Adolf Eichmann and brought him to Berlin. Eichmann was singled out because he had forced 145,000 Austrian Jews out of Austria. Eichmann was also thought to be an "expert" in Jewish matters. Before the war, Eichmann had visited Palestine and studied the Jewish religion and the Hebrew language. Heydrich and Himmler gave Eichmann the task of being head of the "Jewish desk" in Berlin. They gave him near absolute power over the fate of the Jewish people in Germany and in all the conquered lands. From behind his desk in a small office in Berlin, Eichmann made the decisions that cost nearly 6 million Jews their lives.

EICHMANN AND HEYDRICH PLAN THE GHETTOS

Together, Eichmann and Heydrich planned the ghettos, knowing they were just stopping places for the Jews. They planned the roundups and the transport of the Jews out of the ghettos, and they also set up a system in which large German industries could "rent" Jewish slaves from the Gestapo. Eichmann even worked out the lies and the threats that were used against the *Judenräte*. As long as the offi-

Heinrich Himmler (left), commander of the SS, with Hitler

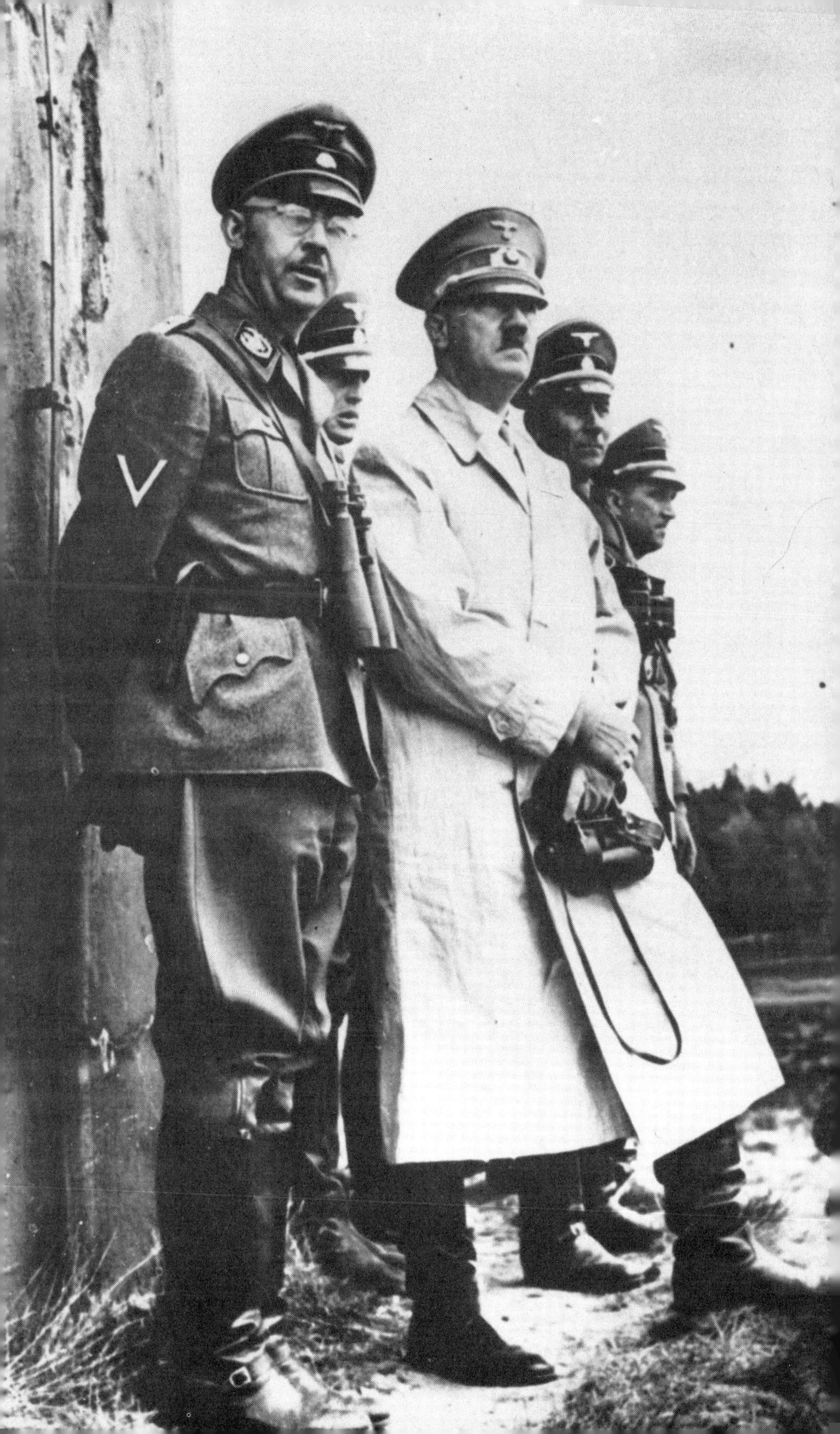

cial Nazi policy was to expel Jews from German soil, Eichmann and Heydrich worked to do just that. They worked just as hard when the Nazis decided to murder every Jew.

THE WANNSEE CONFERENCE

No one is quite certain of the exact moment when the Nazis decided to kill all of the Jews. What seems clear is that the decision was made by January 1942 when many government officials met in the Berlin suburb called Wannsee. At that meeting Heydrich read a report written by Eichmann announcing the "Final Solution of the Jewish Problem." By that time, everyone sitting around the table understood what the words "final solution" meant— the Jews were to be killed.

The biggest question at the Wannsee Conference was exactly how to decide who was a Jew. Jewish religious law says that a Jew is any person born of a Jewish mother or any person who has converted to the Jewish religion. This did not satisfy the Nazis, who were mainly concerned with keeping Aryan blood "pure."

What of the child of a marriage between a Jewish man and an Aryan woman? Jewish law said that the child was not Jewish. But the Nazis said that the blood of such a child was "impure." They said that such children were "dangerous." Aryan blood made them leaders and Jewish blood made them enemies. The Nazis called these half-Jews *Mischlinge*. At Wannsee, the Nazis decided that anyone with one or more Jewish grandparents was a Jew, too, and had to be destroyed. In this way, many Christians came to be called Jews, even though they had been practicing Christianity for two generations!

THE *EINSATZGRUPPEN*

Even as the Wannsee Conference was taking place, Russian Jews were being murdered in special "actions." Groups of *SS* men called *Einsatzgruppen* followed the German army as it marched into Russia. They were the mobile "killing units" of the *SS*. In each town, the *Einsatzgruppen* called on the local rabbi or Jewish town council, demanding a list of all Jews living there. Men, women, and children were rounded up and marched or sent by train, truck, or bus to a nearby forest. There they were forced to undress and stand in line as small groups were taken into a ditch and shot down with machine guns. Nearly 800,000 Russian Jews were murdered by the *Einsatzgruppen*. In one "action," some 35,000 Jews were murdered in the Babi Yar ravine near Kiev. This was the largest single massacre of the war. Still, both Heydrich and Eichmann felt that the destruction was going too slowly. They began to search for a quicker way.

HITLER MAKES A SUGGESTION

It was Hitler who made the next suggestion. As a soldier in World War I, he had been caught in a gas attack. He remembered the bitter, choking feeling of the gas and the fear that gripped him. Gas, he said, was the answer. In 1939, he started a program of putting to death "imperfect Aryans," German children who were mentally ill or physically deformed. Doctors gave these children deadly "shots" in what was termed euthanasia, or "mercy killing." Now Hitler ordered the doctors to experiment with gas. Several German chemical companies went to work trying to find the best gas for putting human beings to death quickly.

At last a gas was chosen to try at Auschwitz: hydrogen cyanide, which the chemical company called Zyklon B. The company that made it had specialized in making poisons for rats and pesticides for insects such as lice. It now went into an additional business—deadly gas for murdering human beings.

THE CONCENTRATION CAMPS

The industry of death was almost ready to begin operation. All that remained was to bring the Jews to it. In Poland and the rest of Europe, concentration camps were set up along railroad lines. Jews were rounded up in the ghettos and shipped out by train. The program began slowly, but after Heydrich's death in May 1942, Eichmann speeded up the transports. In Heydrich's honor, the project was named Operation Reinhard.

The concentration camps were a hundred times worse than the ghettos. But the Jews were told to have hope. Nearly every day, trains arrived at the camps carrying Jews who had traveled for days without food or water. When a train arrived at Auschwitz, loudspeakers blared, ordering people to get off the train and prepare to go to work. It would be good, the officers shouted, for the Jews to go back to work. Men would labor; women would keep house or work with the men; children would go to school. These lies were repeated to each one of the millions who died.

THE FINAL SOLUTION

▲ Concentraton and Extermination camps

⬡ Numbers (in thousands) of Jews murdered

Source: The Anchor Atlas of World History

On the train, the Jews, many sick or wounded, stood closely packed together, afraid to move. German guards often opened fire on them. Some Jews tried to run, while others huddled still closer. The guards shouted, "We know you want to die, but nothing will save you. You will have to go to work."[5] Many Jews were taken in by these words. When they got off the train, they were formed into two lines, women and children in one and men in the other. They went before a table where Nazi officers sat, deciding who would live for a while and who would be put to death immediately.

SURVIVING

Those who were chosen to live found themselves in a kind of hell on earth. All of the camps operated in about the same way. Inside there were the Jewish police—prisoners known as *kapos*—who served the Nazis as other Jews had in the ghettos. There were also German guards (and sometimes Polish and Ukranian guards) always present, ready and willing to beat or shoot anyone who did not obey orders. Thousands of people were crowded into barracks that were designed for hundreds. Often there was only one bathroom, always out of order, for over 400 people. The food was a thin soup that contained almost no nourishment. Some days there was no food at all. Dead bodies littered the paths of the camp while the living fought in the gutter for scraps of garbage to eat. In some camps, roll call was taken every day and sometimes went on for hours,

---

[5] Testimony given at the Eichmann trial. In Gideon Hausner, *Justice in Jerusalem* (New York: Harper & Row, 1966), 167.

Two dying prisoners at Nordhausen concentration camp lie among the dead on the barracks floor. This photo was taken by allied forces after Germany's surrender.

even if it was snowing or raining, hot or cold. There were hospitals and doctors, but there was no medicine.

Within the first few days, thousands would die of hunger, exposure, and disease. Some chose to "run into the wire," that is, take their own lives by throwing themselves against the electrified fences. Still others died of severe beatings, torture, or abuse. Nazi officers sometimes amused themselves by shooting Jews for "target practice." If a person in a barracks escaped, the rest of the Jews in that barracks would immediately be put to death. People who were sick pretended to be well. They knew that if they stopped working, they would be killed.

Life was so terrible in these camps that the Jews turned inward even more than before. They developed a spirit that the guards could not beat out of them and even their hunger could not destroy. Everyone thought of suicide at one time or another, but most of the Jews found strength in their religion or in helping others. Even in this desperate place, they found small ways of sharing and celebrating that made them proud of being Jewish.

THE DEATH CAMPS

For those chosen to die, the next stop was the death camp. Sometimes this was nearby, right next door. Otherwise, there would be a march or train ride to reach it. And sometimes, the prisoners were loaded onto trucks or trains and gassed on the road or along the railroad tracks, never reaching the death camp at all.

Auschwitz was the largest concentration camp. Nearby was the death camp called Birkenau; it was just on the other side of the electrified fence. The Jews were divided.

Men went to one side, while women had their hair shaved off (the hair was used to make blankets for German soldiers). Everyone was told to strip. Naked they were told they were going to the "showers." As they passed through the doorway, they were given bars of soap to make them believe that there was still hope. Most knew the truth. Mothers held their babies close to them. People began to pray; some sang. The *SS* men shoved them into the gas chambers, packing them in so closely that they stood on each other's feet.

The doors and windows were tightly shut. The gas was pumped into the crowded room. The dead had no place to fall. They stood in death as they had in life—families pressed together, holding hands; strangers with their arms around each other. Jewish workers were forced to remove the corpses from the gas chambers and put them into huge furnaces or ovens. The bodies were burned to ashes. The odor of burning flesh rose with the smoke. It was pumped out of chimneys. It could be seen and smelled for miles around.

Nearly 6 million Jews passed through the doors of the death camps. At Auschwitz and Birkenau alone, almost 2 million people were murdered.

THE FINAL "ARYANIZATION"

From the beginning of the anti-Semitic campaign, the Nazis found ways of making themselves and Germany richer at the expense of the Jews. By the end of the war, nearly $9 billion of Jewish money, goods, and property had been collected and given to non-Jews through this legalized theft. The Nazis called it Aryanization.

After the war, civilians view the remains of Jews killed at the Buchenwald camp.

In March 1942, Hitler set up a special staff called the *Einsatzstab* to confiscate the most valuable pieces of art and literature owned by the Jews. The collecting took place as the Jews themselves were being transported to their deaths. The *Einsatzstab* also collected Jewish Bibles and copies of Jewish holy books. Nearly 6 million volumes were brought to a mansion near Frankfurt to be studied by Nazi scholars who wanted to prove to the world how dangerous Jews and their ideas were.

The *Einsatzstab* soon realized that the works of art were more valuable than the books. These were given to Nazi leaders or placed in German museums. In only three years, the Nazis collected more than 21,000 works of art—paintings, drawings, miniatures, sculptures, medallions, and antiques. Jewish apartments were sometimes left fully furnished and given to Nazi officers as places to live.

The Nazis even found ways to make money from dead Jews. In Operation Reinhard, starting in 1942, gold fillings were taken from the teeth of Jewish corpses. Wedding rings and any other jewelry was removed from dead hands and necks. Shoes and clothing were sorted for size and resold to non-Jews. (Sometimes customers would complain when they found bullet holes in their new coats or bloodstains on dresses they bought for their children.)

Suitcases, thermos bottles, baby bottles, shawls, and blankets were collected from those entering concentration or death camps and resold. Eyeglasses and monocles were plucked from dead eyes. Artificial limbs were "recovered" from Jews who no longer needed them. Sometimes the bones of the dead Jews were ground up to make phosphate, and the little fat they had was used to make soap.

Even Jewish cemeteries were plundered. Iron gates and funeral monuments were resold. Tombstones were used to pave German streets. In October 1943, Himmler wrote, "The wealth they had we have taken from them. . . . This is a glorious page in our history, never before, never again to be written."[6]

---

[6]Lucy S. Dawidowicz, *A Holocaust Reader* (New York: Behrman House, 1976), 133.

8

ESCAPE AND RESCUE

As soon as World War II began, the Jews living in Europe became trapped. Before the war, in the late 1930s, thousands of Jews fled Germany by car or train or even on foot. Most went to nearby countries, where the German armies later caught up with them. Some traveled longer distances, setting out for North or South America or for Palestine (now Israel). Even for these people, there were unexpected troubles.

THE BOAT PEOPLE

The ship *St. Louis* set sail from Europe on May 13, 1939. Aboard were 930 German Jews bound for the United States; unfortunately, only 700 of these people had immigration numbers. In those days, anyone who wished to settle in the United States needed an immigration number. These were given to a certain number of people from each foreign country. But so many Jews were coming from Germany that there were no more immigration numbers left

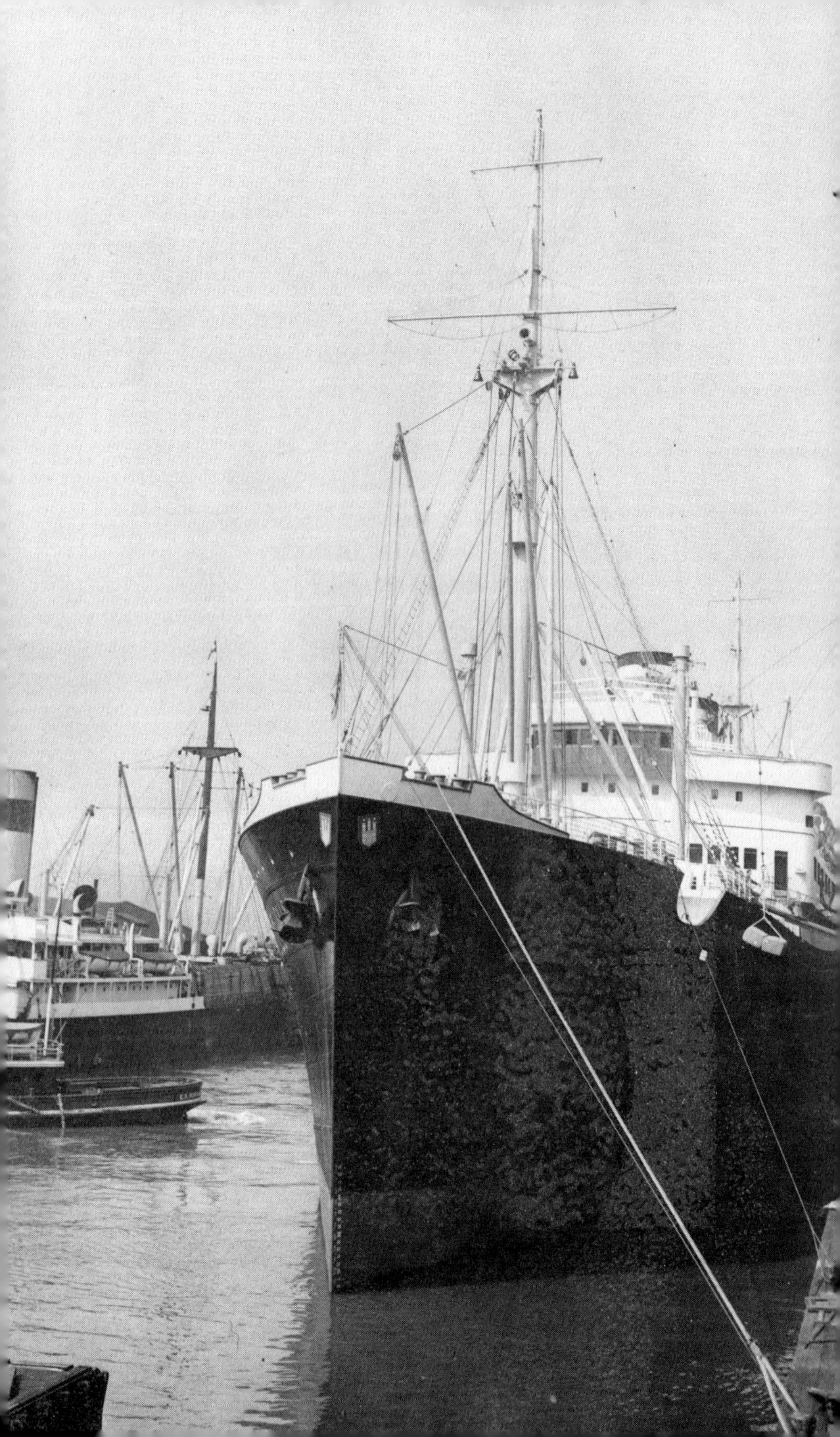

for Germans. Even for those with immigration numbers, there was a waiting period of at least three years before they would be allowed into the United States. Knowing this, the German Jews on the *St. Louis* planned to wait in Cuba. The Cuban government, however, decided that only thirty people would be allowed to come off the boat. Messages were sent to the United States, but the U.S. government refused to accept any of the German Jews before their time. In the end, the *St. Louis* had to set sail again for Germany!

Jewish leaders begged government after government for help, even as the *St. Louis* made its way back across the Atlantic. No government would accept all 930 Jews, but four countries—France, Great Britain, Belgium, and Holland—finally agreed to divide the refugees among them. Thus, many of the refugees who temporarily found safety in Europe were again trapped when the German armies overran Belgium, Holland, and France.

Other boatloads of Jews reached distant ports only to be turned away. One ship, the *Struma,* carried 769 Jews from port to port for seventy-four days, finally sinking in the Black Sea a few miles from Istanbul, Turkey. All but two of the passengers were drowned.

Meanwhile, Jews escaping on foot were also turned away from country after country. Few places would accept any Jewish refugees. Switzerland passed a law forbidding

The St. Louis *docked in New York before it had to go back to Europe.*

Jews from crossing its borders. Great Britain and Australia accepted a few Jews but then closed their borders to all of the rest. France, before it was conquered, refused to accept any Jews, saying it already had too many. So the escaping Jews looked to Palestine, where there was a large Jewish community anxious to welcome them. But Palestine was then controlled by Great Britain, and the British refused to allow Jews to enter.

REFUSAL TO RESCUE JEWS

By August 1942, the Nazis had killed almost 1.5 million Jews. One American Jewish leader, Rabbi Stephen S. Wise of New York City, went again and again to the U.S. State Department, bringing reports of the Nazi plan for the "Final Solution" and proving that Jews were being sent to death camps. It was not until November that the State Department accepted the fact that Jews were being murdered. Even then very little was done. The Allies sent out a declaration in December saying that the Nazis would be punished after the war for what they had done to the Jews.

Stephen Wise wanted to save Jewish lives. In 1943, he worked out a secret plan for rescuing 70,000 Jews. Money was to be put in Swiss banks for bribing Germans to save Jews. President Franklin D. Roosevelt approved the plan, but the British Foreign Office stopped it, saying that they would not know what to do with the Jews who were rescued. Other plans failed, too. When the Nazis saw that the war was going badly for them, Eichmann agreed to "sell" thousands of Hungarian Jews in return for coffee, tea, soap, and trucks. The Allies refused to allow this exchange, saying that stocking the Nazis would only make

Rabbi Stephen S. Wise, an outspoken American Jewish leader, tried to save European Jewish lives.

the war last longer. Some 100,000 Hungarian Jews might have been "bought" from Eichmann and saved. Instead, most of them died.

In effect, the Allies refused to help the Jews of Europe. They said that fighting the war was the most important thing. After the war, they said, the world would be safe for everyone. This did not console Jewish leaders. They knew that few Jews would be left at the war's end. One Jewish leader suggested that the Allies bomb the railroads and the death camps, to slow down the killing. The British replied that only military targets would be bombed, though in the end the Allies also bombed German cities.

THE CHURCH AND THE JEWS

For a while, the Jewish leaders hoped that the official churches of Islam, Buddhism, and Christianity might speak out against the slaughter of innocent human beings. Above all, the Jews hoped that the Pope, the most prominent Christian leader, would publicly speak out for the victims and against the Nazi government. He never did this. Perhaps he was afraid of what might happen to the Catholics of Germany. Or perhaps he was afraid that Hitler might win the war.

On the other hand, many religious leaders spoke out, and some even took action. Those inside conquered lands—especially the Catholics in France—risked their lives doing so. Many nunneries hid Jewish children who pretended to be Catholic to escape the Nazis. Hundreds of Jewish children were saved in this way. In Belgium, Protestant and Catholic priests did all they could to help the Jews, especially Jewish children. One priest, Father André, arranged to hide many children. He even continued their Jewish education rather than educating them as Christians.

THE RIGHTEOUS FEW

In addition to help from members of the churches, many Jews were aided by other European non-Jews, who risked their lives to help. In Holland, Jews were hidden in homes of non-Jewish neighbors. In fact, so many Jews were hidden in this way that the Nazis often had to make house-to-house searches to round them up. The French resistance forces made the smuggling of Jewish refugees across the Alps and Pyrenees mountains a part of their regular activities. And the Nazis were once forced to arrest 400 French policemen who refused to round up and arrest Jews.

Inside Germany, the Confessing Church used its buildings as way stations, hiding Jews as they made their way to safety in Switzerland. And 5,000 Dutch Jews and several thousand German Jews were hidden by non-Jews in the cities of Berlin and Hamburg—in the heart of the Nazi empire.

One Dutchman, Joop Westerweel, led group after group of Dutch Jewish youngsters on marches to the foot of the Pyrenees, where they crossed into Spain. In the summer of 1944, he was captured by the Nazis and executed. There were even rare moments when a whole town or nation raised its voice to help. In the wine country of France, an entire town worked to rescue Jews. In Bulgaria, when the Nazis came to round up the Jews, people gathered in the streets yelling, "We want the Jews back!"

THE GREATEST RESCUE: DENMARK

The most dramatic story of rescue involved Denmark. When the Germans entered Denmark to "protect" it, a Nazi official spoke to King Christian X of Denmark about the "Jewish problem." Christian replied, "We have no Jewish problem in our country. The Jews are a part of the Danish nation."[7] In October 1943, the Nazis decided to round up the Danish Jews to send them to the death camps. The Danes heard about the intended roundup, and the gov-

---

[7] Philip Friedman, *Their Brothers' Keepers* (New York: Holocaust Library, 1978), 40.

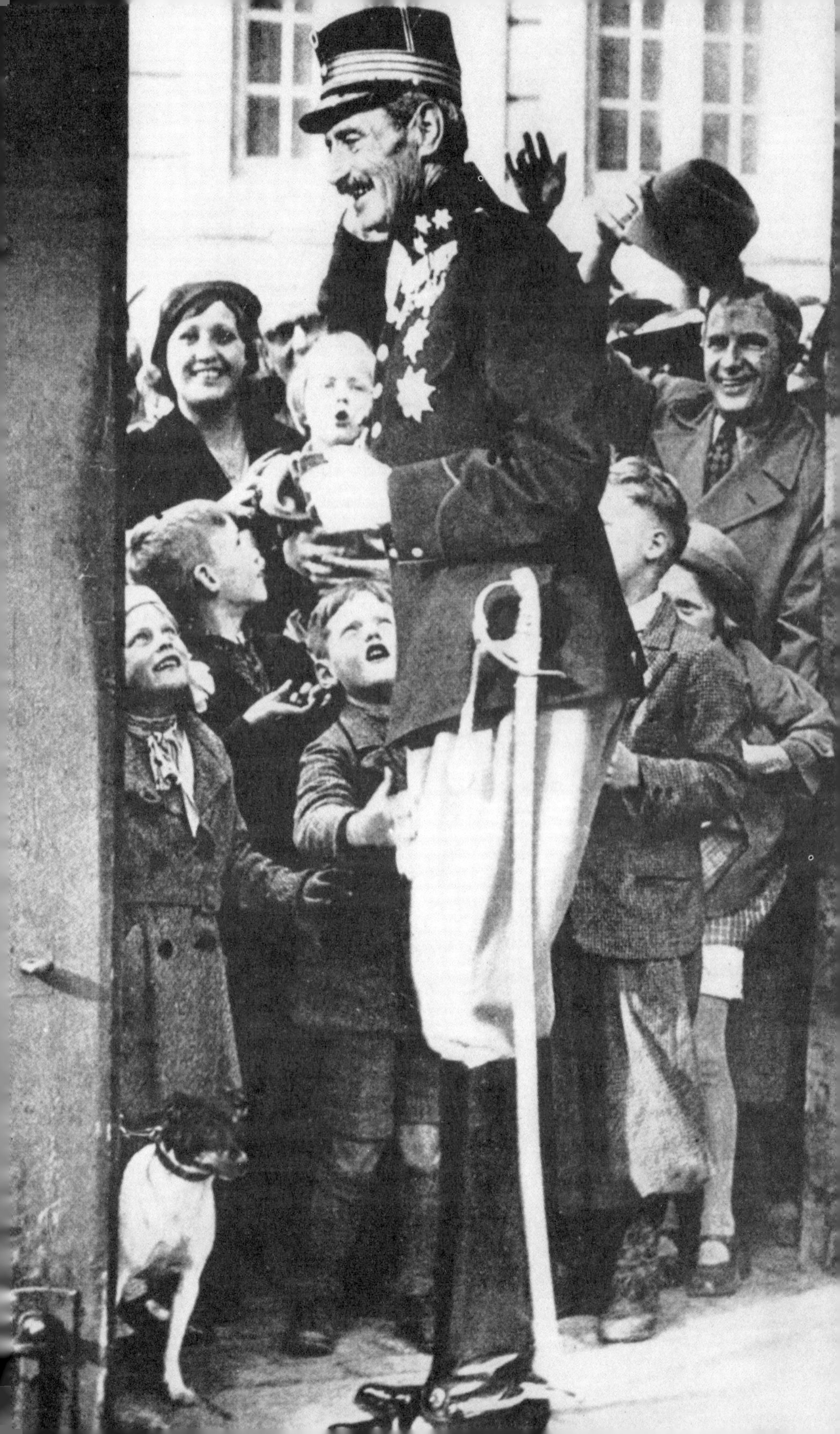

ernment sent a protest to the Germans. Not waiting for an answer, the Danish people organized themselves, with Sweden's help, into a nation of rescuers.

Sweden had not fallen to the Nazis, and now its government offered safety to the Jews of Denmark. The only problem was how to ferry thousands of Jews across the 15-mile (24-km) stretch of water between the two countries. Despite the risks, the people of Denmark took on this enormous task. Jews were hidden in their neighbors' houses, then smuggled in small groups into the fishing villages along the Danish coast. From there they were taken in fishing boats, pleasure craft, and sailboats across the channel to Sweden. Over 7,000 Danish Jews—nearly the entire Jewish population of Denmark—were saved in this rescue.

The Danes also refused to make a profit on Jewish property. They protected Jewish homes throughout the war. When Jews returned to Denmark after the war, they found their homes and apartments as they had left them, their bank accounts untouched.[8]

Christian X, the king of Denmark, and the Danish people helped save most of the Jews in Denmark. The tall, popular monarch was called "the people's king."

[8] Raul Hilberg, *The Destruction of the European Jews* (New York: Franklin Watts, 1973), 363.

JEWISH EFFORTS
TO RESCUE THE JEWS

In 1943, the British finally agreed to help in a rescue effort. Thirty-two young Jews from Palestine were parachuted behind German lines. One of these was Hannah Senesh, who volunteered to help because her mother was still in Hungary. She and two others landed in Yugoslavia and secretly contacted the Hungarian freedom fighters. But the Hungarians were anti-Semites and turned the three Jews over to the Nazis. One escaped. The other two were tortured and put to death. Later, Hannah Senesh's diary was discovered, and her name and story became a legend. Her friend who escaped managed to save thousands of Jewish lives. Most of the others were not so lucky. Seven of the original thirty-two were killed. Many were captured and tortured by the Nazis.

The sad fact is that, taken altogether, the rescue efforts of nations, towns, clergy, and individuals—Jews and non-Jews alike—saved only a few thousand lives. The Nazis managed to take 6 million.

REVOLT AND FREEDOM

Nearly 6 million Jews were killed in what historians have called the Holocaust. A holocaust is a great raging fire that consumes in its path all that lives. In the Bible, the word *holocaust* is also used as the name for a kind of sacrifice, a burnt offering. The Holocaust was the largest loss of life ever suffered by any one people.

After the war, when people learned that 6 million Jews died in the Holocaust, they asked, why did so many Jews go to the camps without a struggle? Why didn't the Jews fight back? It took many years for the whole story of the Holocaust to be told; in fact, we are still learning more about it today, a generation after it happened. The truth is that the Jews *did* fight back. They fought back not in just one place but in many places, and not in just one way but in many ways.

GHETTO REVOLTS

On July 18, 1942, the Jews in the small ghetto of Nieswiez threw homemade sulfuric acid into the faces of German policemen. When more policemen came, the Jews turned a machine gun on them that had been smuggled into the ghetto piece by piece. Then they set the ghetto aflame, burning their own homes. The Germans took revenge by hunting down and killing every last rebel. Then they murdered all of the Jews who had lived in the ghetto. This was the Nazi answer to revolts. In many cases, the only records we have of these kinds of revolts are the records kept by the Nazis themselves. Not a single Jew escaped to tell the tale.

In most ghettos it was the young people—especially Zionists—who organized the revolts. The Zionists were those who wanted a Jewish state in Palestine. They were the first to believe the rumors about the concentration and death camps. They smuggled guns into the ghettos and trained themselves to fight. Young women often acted as messengers, slipping out of one ghetto into another, carrying news and smuggling weapons. As time went on, everyone knew the truth. Millions had already been killed. More and more, the residents of ghettos such as Krakow, Warsaw, Vilna, and Bialystok prepared to revolt. At Krakow, the Jews organized a surprise attack outside the ghetto, trapping the *SS* where they gathered to drink and talk. The German losses were heavy. But as the fighting continued, most of the Jews were captured and shot. Many of these young people might have succeeded in escaping from the ghettos, but they wanted to stay with their families. They did not want to leave behind the old, the sick, and the children. So they died fighting.

THE WARSAW GHETTO UPRISING

The best-known ghetto revolt took place in Warsaw. Plans were made for it in advance. Guns and ammunition were smuggled in, and bottles were filled with gasoline to make homemade bombs called Molotov cocktails that could be set aflame and thrown. In January 1943, with only 70,000 Jews left in the Warsaw ghetto, a small revolt broke out. Heinrich Himmler himself came to see what was happening. He decided that it was time to destroy the whole ghetto.

When German tanks rolled into the Warsaw ghetto on April 19, 1943, 1,000 Jewish fighters were ready for them. They had 3 machine guns, about 80 rifles, hand grenades, Molotov cocktails, and perhaps 300 pistols and revolvers. There were more than 2,000 fully armed German troops. The Jews blew up the German tanks, blocking the entrance to the ghetto and forcing the Germans to retreat.

The Germans returned with more soldiers, tanks, artillery, and flamethrowers. The fighting grew heavier. Jews were driven from the streets, and the fight went on from house to house. The Jews fought on until they had no more ammunition. Then they hid in tunnels they had dug beneath the buildings. The fighting was so heavy, the German commander had to send for more troops. A week passed, then two more. On May 8, the Germans finally reached the central command post of the Jewish fighters. Over a hundred fighters fell in that one building. Many took their own lives so that they would not fall into German hands.

Still the battle continued; it was not over until June, when the ghetto was burned to the ground. A few Jews escaped through the sewers. The Warsaw ghetto had been destroyed. But the Jews had proved—to themselves and to the whole world—that they could fight as fiercely as any people on earth.

Polish rebels, half starved, come out of their hiding places after the Warsaw ghetto uprising.

PARTISANS

Many of the Jews who escaped—from the ghettos, the trains, and the camps—joined the underground movements that existed in every land controlled by the Germans. These groups of freedom fighters were made up mostly of young men and women. They stole or bought guns and attacked the Germans whenever and wherever possible. In Poland they gathered in the forests and became "partisan" fighters. They came out of hiding to strike at the Nazis, then fled to the forests where the German army could not easily follow them. Some Polish partisan groups allowed Jews to join them. Other groups were anti-Semitic, hating the Jews almost as much as the Nazis did. In some cases, the Jews created their own partisan groups. Even though the partisans were not very successful against the huge German war machine, it was the dream of many a young man or woman in the ghetto and the concentration camp to escape and become a partisan.

RESISTANCE IN THE CAMPS

Those who could not, or would not, escape dreamed of revolt. The first problem was always how to get weapons. This was an even greater problem in the camps than it was in the ghettos. At least the ghetto residents had some contact with the outside world. In the camps, the Jews were entirely cut off. In Treblinka, one Jew managed to get a duplicate key for the armory in which the Germans stored their guns and ammunition. The armory was taken, and 200 Jews armed themselves. The gas chambers, the railroad station, and the guards' barracks were all set ablaze in minutes. The barbed wire fence was cut and torn away, and people fled toward the forests. But the Nazis called for more soldiers. Hundreds of Jews were killed before they could even reach the forests. Only a few escaped to tell of the revolt at Treblinka, but word of it led to revolts in other camps.

Women fought as bravely as men. At Auschwitz, a Jewish woman named Mala became a symbol of courage and defiance. Mala stole an *SS* uniform and official documents telling of the slaughter at the camp. She escaped, only to be recaptured, sent back to Auschwitz, and tortured. The Nazis decided to hang her in front of the whole camp. When the *SS* executioner stepped close, Mala slapped her across the face. "I fall a heroine," she yelled, "and you will die a dog."[9] In 1944, there was a revolt in the women's camp at Auschwitz. Using dynamite that had been smuggled in stick by stick by girls who worked in the ammunition factory, the women blew up one of the furnaces. As usual, the cost of revolt was high. All of the women who had taken part in the revolt were captured, tortured, and finally hanged.

SPIRITUAL RESISTANCE: THE COURAGE TO DIE

When revolt was impossible, many Jews met death calmly. Religious Jews said it was a sacrifice, *al kiddush hashem,* "to glorify God." In the end, they believed, God would come to the aid of the Jewish people, and the Germans would be defeated and punished. As the *Einsatzgruppen*

---

[9] Testimony given at the Eichmann trial. In Gideon Hausner, *Justice in Jerusalem* (New York: Harper & Row, 1966), 191.

stood ready to shoot Russian Jews in the forests, rabbis or community leaders would talk to their people or lead them in singing. In the camps, Jews continued to study Judaism with rabbis and teachers. They celebrated on Jewish holidays, even saving bits of fat that they could have eaten to light as Sabbath "candles." Although they were being put to death because they were Jews, they resisted by remaining Jewish to the end.

German documents captured after the war show that Jews went to the gas chambers with prayers on their lips or voices raised in song. Even crowded into the gas chambers, individuals spoke bravely to the group, saying that the Germans would soon be defeated and Judaism would survive. Nazi officers were amazed by this. They could not understand how a people they thought so "inferior" could die with such dignity.

THE LAST MARCH

When the Germans realized that they were losing the war and that Russian troops were nearing the camp at Auschwitz in Poland, an order was given for the Jewish prisoners to be marched back to Germany. It was a cold January day in 1945. Nearly 55,000 prisoners, all that remained of the millions sent to Auschwitz, were marched out of the camp. There was no food for them, and they were weak. Many fell along the roadsides. The *SS* men shot them where they fell. Some days there were as many as 500 shootings. The Jews were forced to spend nights in stables or in the open. One night, they were placed in a tunnel, and its end was closed up. Many suffocated from lack of air. The next morning, there were a thousand dead in the tunnel. Those who survived the last march were put in concentration camps inside Germany. They were still there when the Allied troops found them—skeletons, starved and shrunken, with huge eyes staring out of swollen eyesockets. It was hard to believe that they had once been healthy, normal human beings. Many were too weak to rise from the wooden shelves that the Nazis called beds.

In the world of the Holocaust, survival itself was the greatest form of resistance. As Gerda Klein, one of the survivors, wrote, "It seemed almost a luxury to die, to go to sleep and never wake up again."[10]

---

[10] Gerda Weissmann Klein, *All But My Life* (New York: Hill and Wang, 1957), 167.

10

THE END

GERMANY'S DEFEAT

On June 6, 1944, the Allies landed troops on the beaches at Normandy, France. By midnight, the Germans had lost the battle and the Allies had a firm foothold in Europe. In July, the Russians pushed forward toward Poland. The Germans retreated. By September, American troops stood on German soil. Hitler's world was closing in on him.

In one last desperate attack, Hitler sent troops into the Ardennes forest in France, trying to wedge apart the American and British armies. This was the Battle of the Bulge, the fiercest and bloodiest battle of World War II. It was over by January 16, 1945. No one really won the battle, but Hitler's army suffered such heavy losses that the Germans never recovered.

HITLER'S DEATH

Hitler hid in a bunker designed and built for him beneath Berlin. Most of the Nazi leaders left Berlin as it was being surrounded by Allied troops in April. Hitler refused to leave his bunker. On April 30, Adolf Hitler shot and killed himself. By his own orders, his body was taken outside the bunker and burned. The day before, Hitler had written out a final statement to the German people. Nothing had changed for him, he said. It was the Jews who wanted the war, he said. "Above all," he wrote, "I call on the leaders of the nation and the people to uphold the racial [anti-Semitic] laws to their full extent and to oppose mercilessly the universal poisoner of all peoples, International Jewry."[11]

Hitler died as he had lived, believing that his real war was not against other nations but against the Jewish people. The Holocaust—the death of 6 million Jews—was no accident; it was the careful plan of a criminal with the powers of an emperor. Moreover, the murder of 6 million people could not be carried out by one man alone. Thousands of Germans had taken part, and they had been helped by scores of other Europeans.

A DEAFENING SILENCE

After the war, such people would say that they had not known what was happening in the camps. Germans chose to forget about *Kristallnacht,* about stealing from German Jews, about roundups in Germany. They said the slaughter happened in faraway places. They asked, how could they know what was happening to the Jews of Austria, Poland, Czechoslovakia, Hungary, France, Belgium, Luxembourg, Holland, Italy, Rumania, Greece, and Yugoslavia?

---

[11] Lucy S. Dawidowicz, *The War Against The Jews: 1933–1945* (New York: Bantam Books, 1976), 28.

Even outside of Germany, non-Jews grew silent about what they had seen and what they knew. Yet the truth was all around—in cities and in towns alike. During the war, they had seen Jews being marched out of the ghettos to work in factories, to clean streets, to work in mines. Homes were filled with art, furniture, bedding, and clothes that came from Jewish neighbors. What had happened could not be covered up. Those who took part in it wanted to forget it, but it could not be forgotten. They could be silent, but they could not silence the blood that cried everywhere from the ground.

THOSE WHO STOOD BY

Those who worked in the concentration and death camps, those who owned or ran the factories that "rented" Jewish slaves from the *Gestapo,* those who served as guards at ghetto gates and in concentration and death camps, those who served in the *Einsatzgruppen* murdering Jews in the east—all of these people took part in the murder. Even those who lived in the towns near the death camps, smelling the death and watching the smoke rise from the tall chimneys, were partly to blame. They might have stopped the murder, or at least slowed down the machinery of death, if they had chosen to act. They could have rescued Jews if they had chosen to help. Instead, they chose silence. And afterward, they chose to forget because the truth was just too horrible to recall.

In the end, the Nazis tried to hide what they had done to the Jews. They tried to plow the camps under, to bury the thousands of corpses that lay piled high beside the ovens, to destroy the careful lists they kept in the "books of the

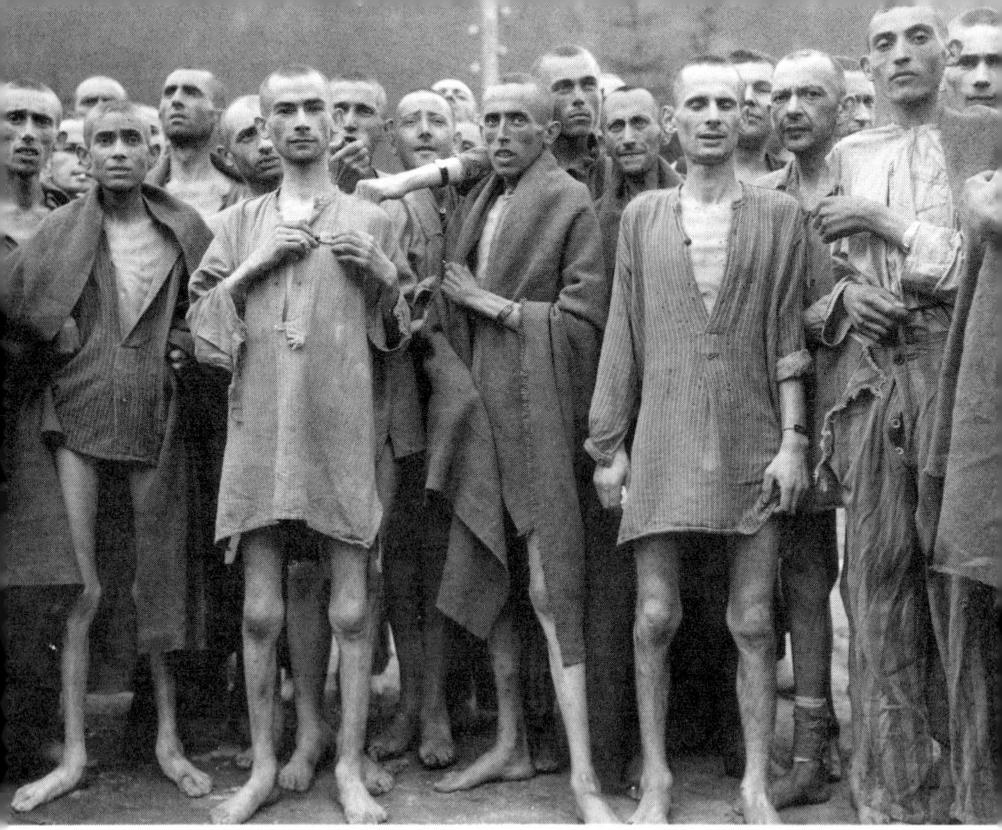

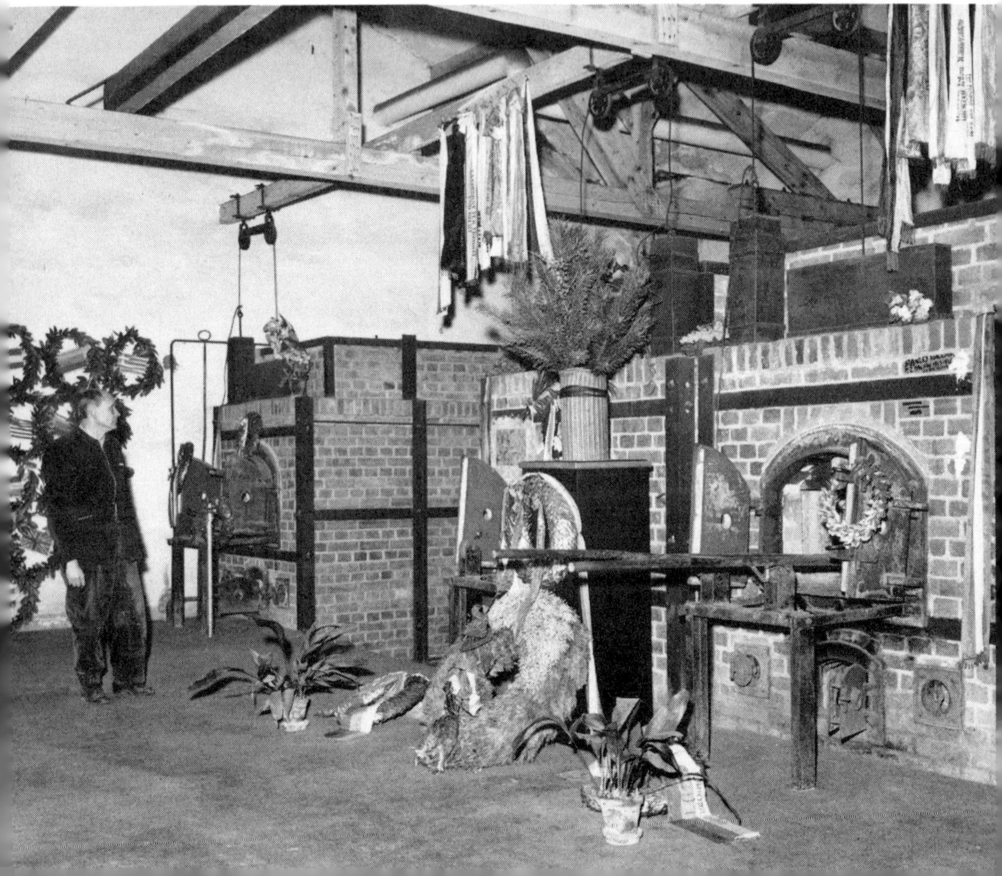

dead." Eichmann worked feverishly to destroy the records in his central office. But the Allied troops came too quickly. Records were captured. Camps were still standing. Some of the Nazi lists of the dead had survived the burning. Corpses still lay in the sunlight exposing the horror. And there were still survivors to tell the story.

THE TRIALS

In 1943, the Allies promised that Nazi war criminals would be brought to trial after the war. These trials were held in Nuremberg, Germany, beginning on November 20, 1945. They lasted for 403 court sessions. They were the largest war-crime trials in history. The top Nazi officers were allowed to choose their own lawyers. Many world-famous lawyers were appointed to help in their defense. And equally famous lawyers from among the Allied nations formed the prosecution.

Above: *starved prisoners, nearly dead from hunger, at one of the concentration camps in Austria. The prisoners were liberated by American soldiers in May 1945.* Below: *years after the war, a former camp prisoner looks at the ovens of Dachau, where thousands of people were cremated. Floral wreaths honor those who were burned there.*

The Holocaust was hardly mentioned. Most of the Nazi leaders stood trial for "crimes against peace." They were accused of breaking laws that existed long before the war began.

The defense said that the Nazi leaders were only doing their duty to the German state. But the judges advanced a new idea—that some laws are "international moral laws," including the laws against murder and enslavement. Duty to these laws, they said, comes first.

The defense then said that in Nazi Germany one man—Adolf Hitler—gave all of the orders. Hitler was *der Führer,* the Leader. His orders had to be obeyed on pain of death. This was called the *Führer-prinzip,* the "leadership principle." They claimed that, in all of Germany, only Hitler was guilty. The judges did not agree. They had copies of orders signed by every top leader, not just by Hitler. Moreover, they repeated, it is a crime to obey any order "which is clearly a crime against peace," no matter who gives the order.

In the end, three men were set free. Nineteen were found guilty. Twelve were hanged. The Nuremberg trials lasted nearly a year.

Dozens of smaller trials followed. Many who had been in charge of ghettos, concentration camps, and death camps were tried. Nazi doctors who used Jews as guinea pigs in unspeakable experiments were tried. Officers who had tortured Jewish men and raped Jewish women were tried. And there were separate trials for the officers and leaders of the *Einsatzgruppen.*

The results were rather disappointing. In the Allied countries, many people knew nothing about the "Final Solution"—the murder of 6 million Jews and the plan to kill all Jews everywhere. To this day, many are still not aware that the Nazis wanted to use the same plan against millions of non-Jews. They had tried to destroy the Gypsy people entirely. They had murdered Russian, Polish, and Slav civilians, saying their blood was "inferior." Nazi "euthanasia" programs took the lives of the old, the sick, the lame, the physically deformed, and the mentally handicapped—German and non-German alike. Yet, for many years after the Nuremberg trials, most people remained ignorant of what the Nazis had done.

THE EICHMANN TRIAL

In the confusion just after the war, some high-ranking Nazis escaped. They hid in Russia, in North and South America, and elsewhere. When the state of Israel was established in 1948, a special section of its secret service set out to find these Nazis and bring them to justice. They were helped by a few Jewish survivors of the Holocaust. The "Nazi hunters," people such as Simon Wiesenthal and Tuviah Friedman, had sworn to search for guilty Nazis and bring them to justice. When former Nazi leaders were found in Europe, their names were given to the authorities, and some were brought to trial.

But in many places—especially South America—the Nazis were welcome. The governments refused to arrest them. In May 1960, after a long search, the Israeli secret service located Adolf Eichmann in Argentina. Eichmann had been the Nazi official in charge of the "Final Solution." Knowing that the government of Argentina would not help, they kidnapped Eichmann and took him to Israel. When the announcement was made that Eichmann would be tried in Israel, it seemed that the attention of the world had been captured along with Eichmann.

Eichmann's trial lasted nearly nine months, from April to December of 1961. On television and radio and in the newspapers of the world, the story of the Holocaust was told in detail for the first time. And the people of the world were finally ready to hear it—to learn about the ghettos, the camps, and the ovens. Eichmann was found guilty, sentenced to die, and hanged. His ashes were scattered over the Mediterranean Sea outside Israeli waters.

THE TRIALS GO ON

The story does not end there. More Nazi criminals have since been located and tried. In 1974, Elizabeth Holtzman, a representative from New York to the U.S. Congress, learned that Nazi criminals were living freely and openly in the United States. Although the U.S. government was not trying to hide Nazis, no one in the government had the power to locate them. And there was no law in the United States under which they could be brought to trial! Finally, in 1977, Representative Holtzman persuaded the Justice Department to form a special investigating unit. Hundreds of cases were brought to light, and more than twenty former Nazis have been brought to trial for lying about their past on their citizenship papers. A few have been convicted. Their punishment is losing their U.S. cit-

Adolf Eichmann giving evidence at his trial in Jerusalem, Israel

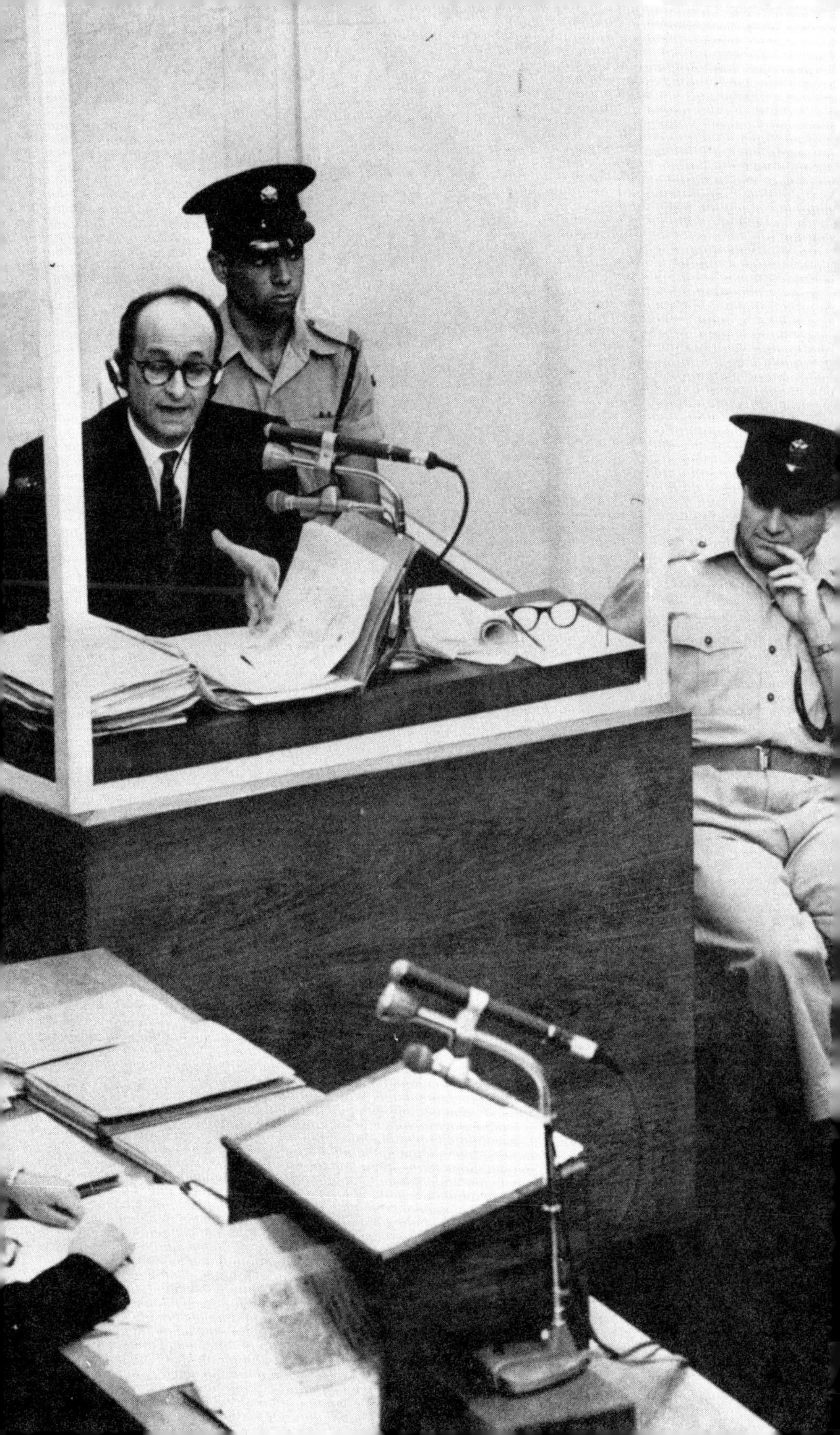

izenship and being sent back to the country they came from. It is then up to that country to put them on trial for their crimes during the war.

The Nazi hunters continue to look for others. Each trial tells us more and more about what happened and how it happened. But no trial can tell us *why* it happened—why people *allowed* it to happen. For the answer to those questions, we must all look into our hearts. Would we let our neighbors be taken without speaking out? Would we let them be put to death without trying to rescue them? Would we let another Holocaust happen?

WHAT DOES IT MEAN TO BE HUMAN?

GENOCIDE: A DEFINITION

The word *genocide* was coined in 1944 by Raphael Lamkin, a lawyer and a Polish Jew. It is a combination of the Greek word *genos* (meaning "race," "group," or "tribe") and the Latin ending *cide* (meaning "killing.") The Allies, led by Franklin D. Roosevelt and Winston Churchill, shared a dream that the nations of the world would join together after World War II in an international effort to maintain peace and security. Their creation, the United Nations, was organized to protect the rights of all people, no matter what their sex, language, religion, or race.

From the first meeting of the General Assembly, the United Nations had to deal with the issues raised by the Holocaust. Based on the results of the trials at Nuremberg, the UN set forth two resolutions. One declared that the nations of the world should bring to trial those accused of war crimes and crimes against humanity. The second declared genocide to be "a crime under international law."

This UN resolution brought the word *genocide* into international law for the first time.

Two years later, the United Nations approved a "Genocide Convention," an international treaty that defined just what was meant by the word. Genocide was defined as acts committed with intent to destroy, in whole or in part, a national, ethnic, racial, or religious group. Genocide, according to this treaty, includes killing members of a group, causing serious bodily or mental harm to them, forcing them to live in ways that would cause them suffering and death, preventing births among them, or removing their children from them. And the treaty says these are crimes not only in times of war but in times of peace as well.

After it was approved by the United Nations, it remained for each individual nation to approve the Genocide Convention. By 1951 enough members had approved it so that it "officially" took force. But many important nations, including the United States, have never approved it. The United States has not signed because it does not wish to give other nations reason to question actions taken inside the United States. This failure to sign shows just how weak international law really is.

THE END OF THE STORY IS THE END OF SILENCE

How, then, can nations prevent something like the Holocaust from happening again? Learning about it, reading about it, and studying it will help. Understanding the past enables us to build a better future. This was seen in postwar Germany, especially. For many years, the Holocaust

Auschwitz, the concentration camp in Poland where 2 million people were killed, is a reminder of the horror of the Holocaust.

was a forbidden topic in Germany. It was not mentioned in German textbooks, no one spoke about it, and no one learned about it. Suddenly, when the Eichmann trial began, a whole generation of German children was shocked. The children could hardly believe that their fathers and mothers had been a part of the Hitler Youth, or that their grandparents had taken part in *Kristallnacht* or in the mass murder of Jews. But the Holocaust is a fact of modern history, and now all of us—even the young people of Germany—must face that fact. It could happen anywhere, even in nations that think of themselves as highly "civilized." Learning about it can help to prevent it.

PEOPLE MUST SPEAK OUT FOR ONE ANOTHER

But just learning about it is not enough. People must also stand up for one another. We must see through propaganda, resist blackmail and lies. We must ask what words really mean when they are spoken. The Nazis used *euphemisms*, "code words," to hide what they were doing. They said "Final Solution" and meant murder; they said "transports" and meant railroad rides to death camps; they said "work" and meant death. We must know what our leaders are really saying when they speak. Are they using words to mask what they are doing? We must speak out against wrong and refuse to be silent.

After the war a Protestant pastor, Martin Niemoeller, was one of several clergymen who signed a document declaring that the Christians of Germany shared guilt with the Nazis for what had happened to the Jewish people. Niemoeller had been one of the courageous few in Germany who spoke out when the Nazis tried to control the Christian churches. In 1945, he wrote:

> *In Germany, the Nazis first came for the Communists and I didn't speak up because I wasn't a Communist. Then they came for the Jews, and I didn't speak up because I was not a Jew. Then they came for the trade unionists and I didn't speak up because I was not a trade unionist. Then they came for the Catholics and I was a Protestant so I didn't speak up. Then they came for me: by that time there was no one left to speak up.*[12]

No people can stand alone. We must all stand together against prejudice and hatred. If today it is a danger to others, tomorrow it will be a danger to us.

CAIN AND ABEL

In a few short sentences, the Bible tells the story of the first murder. Cain kills his brother Abel, and when God asks, "Where is Abel your brother?," Cain answers one question with another, "Am I my brother's keeper?" The answer is yes—we *are* all keepers of one another. Whenever a person is murdered, we must all answer the question, "Why are we not better keepers?"

But the key to this biblical story is found not at the end of it but in its middle. Cain and Abel both bring gifts

---

[12] Quoted in Philip Friedman, *Their Brothers' Keepers* (New York: Holocaust Library, 1978), 100.

to God, but only Abel's gift is accepted. This makes Cain angry. Then God gives Cain advice. He says to Cain, "Evil waits for you by the door, but, if you want, you can defeat it."

Evil is never very far away. It is just outside the door, just around the corner. It is even in our hearts, at times. We are human beings—not the best of things and not the worst of things. But we are very special in one way. If we want, we can defeat evil.

There was once a Holocaust in which one group of people murdered 6 million people because they were different. It could happen again, in a similar way or in another way. But if we want, we can keep it from happening.

A CHRONOLOGY OF THE HOLOCAUST

1933

Jan. 30	Adolf Hitler becomes chancellor of Germany.
Mar. 10	First concentration camp set up at Dachau.
Apr. 1	Hitler proclaims one-day boycott of Jewish shops.
Apr. 7	First anti-Jewish law passed in Germany.

1934

Aug. 3	Hitler declares himself both president and chancellor of the Third Reich.

1935

Sept. 15	First Nuremberg laws remove German citizenship from Jews.
Nov. 14	Germans define a Jew as anyone with three Jewish grandparents, or one with two Jewish grandparents who identifies himself as a Jew.

1937

Jul. 19	Buchenwald concentration camp opens.

1938

Mar. 12	Germany takes over Austria; all anti-Jewish laws immediately in force in Austria.

Aug. 1	Adolf Eichmann sets up Office for Jewish Emigration.
Oct. 28	15,000 Jews forced at gunpoint to cross border into Poland.
Nov. 9	German embassy official, Ernst vom Rath, dies in Paris of bullet wounds received November 7. *Kristallnacht* begins, ending November 10 after enormous destruction to Jewish property in Germany.
Nov. 15	Jewish students expelled from German schools.

1939

Aug. 23	Non-aggression treaty signed between Russia and Germany.
Sept. 1	Germany declares war on Poland.
Sept. 3	World War II begins.
Oct. 12	First Austrian Jews sent by train to Poland.
Nov. 23	Polish Jews ordered to wear the yellow badge containing the Star of David.
Nov. 28	First ghetto set up in Poland at Protrkow.

1940

Feb. 12	First deportation of German Jews to concentration camps.
Apr. 9	Germans occupy Denmark.
May 10	Germany invades Holland, Belgium, and France.
May 20	Concentration camp set up at Auschwitz.
Jun. 22	France surrenders to Germany.
Sept. 27	Japan joins Germany and Italy in Axis powers.
Oct. 2	Warsaw ghetto established.
Nov. 20–24	Hungary, Rumania, and Slovakia join the Axis powers.

1941

Mar.	Eichmann appointed head of Gestapo section for Jewish affairs.
Apr.	Germany occupies Greece and Yugoslavia.
Jun. 22	Germany invades Russia.
Jun.–Dec.	*Einsatzgruppen* begin mass murder of Jews in Russia.
Sept. 1	German Jews ordered to wear the yellow badge.
Sept. 28–29	Massacre of Jews at Babi Yar, near Kiev; 35,000 murdered.
Oct. 14	Mass deportation of Jews to concentration camps begins. Birkenau camp opened as site for extermination of Jews, Gypsies, Poles, Russians, and others.
Oct. 23	Massacre of 19,000 Jews in Odessa.
Dec. 7	Japanese attack Pearl Harbor. United States joins Allies.

1942

Jan. 20	Wannsee Conference. Plans for "Final Solution of the Jewish Problem" revealed.
Mar. 1	Extermination by gas begins at Sobibor camp.
Late Mar.	Deportations to Auschwitz begin.
Jun. 20	All Jewish schools closed.
Jul. 28	Jewish fighting group organized in Warsaw ghetto.
Summer	Deportation of Dutch, Polish, French, Belgian, and Croatian Jews to extermination camps; armed resistance by Jews in ghettos.
Oct. 4	All Jews still in concentration camps in Germany scheduled for transfer to Auschwitz.
Nov.	Allied forces land in North Africa.
Winter	Deportations of Norwegian, German, and Greek Jews to concentration camps. Jewish partisan underground movements resist Germans.

1943

Feb. 2	German advance in Russia stopped at Stalingrad.
Apr. 19	Warsaw ghetto revolt begins. Jewish underground fights until early June.
Jun.	Nazis order destruction of all ghettos in Poland and Russia. Armed resistance begins in many ghettos.
Aug. 2	Armed revolt breaks out in Treblinka extermination camp.
Fall	Large ghettos destroyed at Minsk, Vilna, and Riga. Danes begin effort to rescue Jews in Denmark.
Oct. 14.	Armed revolt breaks out in Sobibor extermination camp.

1944

Mar. 19	Germany occupies Hungary.
May 15	Hungarian Jews deported to death camps.
Jun. 6	Allies invade France.
Jul. 24	Extermination camp at Maidenek liberated by Russian army.
Summer	Ghettos at Kovno, Shavli, and Lodz emptied and destroyed. Inmates sent to concentration camps.
Oct. 7	Revolt at Auschwitz.
Oct. 31	Last Slovakian Jews deported to Auschwitz.
Nov. 2	Last Jews transported from Theresienstadt to Auschwitz.
Nov. 8	Beginning of death marches: 40,000 Jews march from Budapest to Austria.

1945

Jan. 17	Auschwitz abandoned. Last prisoners begin death march toward Germany.
Apr. 6	Prisoners from Buchenwald begin four-day death march.
Apr.	Russian army enters Germany from the east as Allied armies enter from the west.
Apr. 30	Hitler commits suicide.
May 7	Germany surrenders. War in Europe ends.
Aug. 15	Japan surrenders. World War II ends.
Nov. 20	Nuremberg War Crimes Trials begin, ending on October 1, 1946.

FOR FURTHER READING

Altshuler, David A. *Hitler's War Against the Jews.* New York: Behrman House, 1978.

Berri, Claude. *The Two of Us.* New York: William Morrow, 1968.

Cowan, Lore. *Children of the Holocaust.* Des Moines, IA: Meredith, 1968.

Forman, James D. *Nazism.* New York: Franklin Watts, 1978.

Frank, Anne. *The Diary of a Young Girl.* New York: Pocket Books, 1952.

Innocenti, Roberto. *Rose Blanche.* Mankot, MN: Creative Education, 1985.

Klein, Gerda. *Promise of a New Spring: The Holocaust and Renewal.* Chappaqua, NY: Rossel Books, 1981.

Lyttle, Richard B. *Nazi Hunting.* New York: Franklin Watts, 1982.

Meltzer, Milton. *Never to Forget: The Jews of the Holocaust.* New York: Harper & Row, 1976.

Reiss, Johanna. *The Upstairs Room.* New York: Thomas Y. Crowell, 1972.

Romm, J. Leonard. *The Swastika on the Synagogue Door.* Chappaqua, NY: Rossel Books, 1984.

Rossel, Seymour. *The Holocaust.* New York: Franklin Watts, 1981.

Shirer, William. *The Rise and Fall of Adolf Hitler.* New York: Random House, 1961.

Stadtler, Bea. *The Holocaust: A History of Courage and Resistance.* New York: Behrman House, 1973.

Suhl, Yuri. *On the Other Side of the Gate.* New York: Franklin Watts, 1975.

SOURCES CONSULTED

A complete list of sources would be a book unto itself. The following list includes two kinds of sources: those that are broad in scope and those that detail special topics highlighted in the narrative.

Allport, Gordon W. *The Nature of Prejudice.* Cambridge, MA: Addison-Wesley, 1954.

Berkovits, Eliezer. *With God in Hell: Judaism in the Ghettos and Death Camps.* New York: Sanhedrin Press, 1979.

Blum, Howard. *Wanted! The Search for Nazis in America.* Greenwich, CT: Fawcett Crest, 1977.

Bullock, Alan. *Hitler: A Study in Tyranny.* New York: Harper & Row, 1964.

Dawidowicz, Lucy S. *A Holocaust Reader.* New York: Behrman House, 1976.

Dawidowicz, Lucy S. *The War Against the Jews: 1933–1945.* New York: Bantam Books, 1976.

Frank, Anne. *The Diary of a Young Girl.* New York: Pocket Books, 1952.

Friedman, Philip. *Their Brothers' Keepers.* New York: Holocaust Library, 1978.

Gilbert, Martin. *The Holocaust.* New York: Henry Holt, 1985.

Grobman, Alex, and Daniel Landes, eds. *Genocide: Critical Issues of the Holocaust.* Chappaqua, NY: Rossel Books, 1983.

Hausner, Gideon. *Justice in Jerusalem.* New York: Harper & Row, 1966.

Hilberg, Raul. *The Destruction of the European Jews.* New York: Franklin Watts, 1973.

Hitler, Adolf. *Mein Kampf.* New York: Houghton Mifflin, 1943.

Poliakov, Leon. *Harvest of Hate.* New York: Holocaust Library, 1979.

Ringelblum, Emmanuel. *Notes from the Warsaw Ghetto.* New York: McGraw-Hill, 1958.

Smith, Bradley F. *Reaching Judgment at Nuremberg.* New York: New American Library, 1977.

Schoenberner, Gerhard. *The Yellow Star: The Persecution of the Jews in Europe, 1933-1945.* New York: Bantam Books, 1979.

Toland, John. *Adolf Hitler.* New York: Doubleday, 1976.

Yahil, Leni. *The Rescue of Danish Jewry.* Philadelphia: JPSA, 1969.

INDEX

Acton, Lord, 65
André, Father, 84
Anti-Semitism. See Jews
Argentina, 103
Art, 77
Aryan race, 18–19, 28, 30, 68
Auschwitz, 70, 74, 94, 95, 109
Australia, 82
Austria, 39, 66, 100

Babi Yar, 69
Battle of the Bulge, 97
"Beer hall *Putsch*," 17–18
Belgium, 43–45, 81, 84
Berlin (Germany), 85
Bible, 77
Birkenau, 74–75
Blackshirts. See SS
Blitzkrieg, 41, 48
Britain. See Great Britain
Brownshirts, 22, 24, 25
Buchenwald, 76
Buddhism, 84
Bulgaria, 85

Cain and Abel, 111–112

Catholic Church, 50–51, 84
Christianity, 16, 30, 50–51, 68–69, 84, 110–111
Christian X, King, 85–86
Communists, 16, 20, 22, 24–25, 45
Concentration camps, 70–74
   death camps, 74–75
   first, 25
   resistance in, 93–94
   surviving in, 72–74
   women in, 94
Confessing Church, 85
Cuba, 81
Czechoslovakia, 39, 64

Dachau, 25, 100
Denmark, 43, 85–87

Eichmann, Adolf, 66, 68, 69, 70, 82–83, 101, 103–104, 105
Einsatzgruppen, 69, 94, 99, 102
Einsatzstab, 77
England. See Great Britain

Finland, 42–43

France, 41, 42, 43, 45, 81, 82, 84–85
Frank, Anne, 52, 54
Friedman, Tuviah, 103

Gassing, 69–70
Genocide, 107–108
Germany:
  anti-Semitism, 16–17, 28–30
  defeat, 97
  Great Depression, 20
  Hitler as dictator, 23–24
  Jewry before Hitler, 52
  Kristallnacht, 36–38, 98, 110
  laws against Jews, 32–33, 39
  Lebensraum, 19, 39
  Nuremberg laws, 33–35
  postwar, 98, 108, 110
  Treaty of Versailles provisions, 11, 14
Gestapo, 25, 55, 66
Ghettos, 50–64
  culture in, 63–64
  in Czechoslovakia, 64
  Eichmann/Heydrich plan, 66
  government in, 58–61
  Jewish way of life in, 63–64
  Judenräte, 59–60, 66
  lack of revolts, 61–63
  model, 64
  Nazi tactics, 58–60
  in Poland, 54–58, 61
  revolts, 89–92
  roundups, 60–61
  school in, 63
  sickness in, 56, 58
  starvation in, 58
  Warsaw, 56–58, 62, 90–91
Gibraltar, 48
Goebbels, Joseph, 28, 36
Goering, Hermann, 38
Great Britain, 41, 42, 43, 45, 81, 82, 88

Great Depression, 19–20
Greece, 45, 48

Hamburg (Germany), 85
Heine, Heinrich, 52
Hess, Rudolf, 18
Heydrich, Reinhard, 35–36, 38, 55, 65–66, 68, 69, 70
Himmler, Heinrich, 25, 65–66, 67, 78
Hitler, Adolf, 102
  anti-Semitism of, 16–17, 18–19
  background, 14, 16
  "Beer hall *Putsch*," 17–18
  confiscation of Jewish property, 77
  death, 97–98
  as dictator, 23–24
  gassing solution, 69–70
  Jews as scapegoats, 29–30
  Mein Kampf, 18–19, 30
  Nazi party, 17–18, 22, 24–31
  path to power, 20–22
  propaganda use, 28–29
  racism, 18–19, 30–31
  Reichstag fire, 22
  war victories, 43–49
  youth movements, 26–28
Holocaust, 89, 98, 102, 108–110, 113–116
Holtzman, Elizabeth, 104
Hungary, 82–83, 88

Islam, 84
Italy, 45, 48

Japan, 48, 49
Jesus, 16
Jews:
  anti-Semitism, 16–17, 18–19
  confiscation of property, 75, 77–78

— 122 —

Jews (*continued*)
  escape and rescue, 79–88
  "final solution," 68, 82,
    102–103
  first deportations, 35–36
  in Germany before Hitler, 52
  Hungarian, 82–83
  Kristallnacht, 36–38
  last march, 95–96
  laws against in Germany, 32–
    35, 39
  partisans, 93
  Russian, 69
  as scapegoats, 29–30
  separation of, 52–60
  spiritual resistance, 94–95
  See also Ghettos

Kapos, 72
Klein, Gerda, 96
Krakow ghetto, 90
Kristallnacht, 36–38, 98, 110

Lamkin, Raphael, 107
Lebensraum, 19, 39
Luftwaffe, 45, 48

Mahler, Gustav, 52
Mein Kampf, 18–19, 30
Mischlinge, 68
Moscow (USSR), 48

Napoleon Bonaparte, 51–52
National Socialist German Workers'
  party, 17
Nazis, 24–31
  attempts to hide deeds, 99,
    101
  confiscation of Jewish property, 75, 77–78
  elections of 1930, 21
  ghetto tactics, 58–60
  hunters of, 103–106

  membership, 25–28
  party formation, 17
  storm troopers, 17–18, 22
  war trials, 101–106
  youth movements, 26–28
Netherlands, The, 43, 81, 84–85
Niemoeller, Martin, 110–111
Nieswiez ghetto, 89–90
Norway, 43
Nuremberg laws, 33–35
Nuremberg trials, 101–102, 107

Operation Reinhard, 77

Palestine, 82, 90
Poland, 35–36, 39, 41, 42, 54–58,
  93
Portugal, 50
Propaganda, 28–29

Racism, 18–19, 30–31
Red Cross, 64
Reichstag fire, 22
Rhineland, 39
Roosevelt, Franklin D., 82
Russia. *See* Soviet Union

St. Louis (ship), 79–81
Schoenberg, Arnold, 52
Senesh, Hannah, 88
Shtetls, 51, 62
Socialists, 25
Soviet Union, 39, 42–43, 45, 48–
  49, 69
Spain, 48, 50
SS (Schutzestaffel; Blackshirts),
  25, 59, 65–66
State Department (U.S.), 82
Struma (ship), 81
Sweden, 87
Switzerland, 81–82

Textbooks, 26, 31

— *123* —

Theresienstadt, 64
Treaty of Versailles, 11, 14
Treblinka, 93–94

United Nations, 107–108
USSR. *See* Soviet Union

Venice (Italy), 50–51

Wannsee Conference, 68
Warsaw ghetto, 56–58, 62, 90–91

Westerweel, Joop, 85
Wiesenthal, Simon, 103
Wise, Stephen, 82
World War II:
    aftermath, 98–99
    beginnings, 39, 41
    Germany's defeat, 97
    Hitler's victories, 43–49

Zionists, 90
Zyklon B, 70

ABOUT THE AUTHOR

Seymour Rossel is an author and publisher of books and textbooks, a composer of music for the guitar, and a frequent lecturer in the field of education.

He studied history and writing at Southern Methodist University and Jewish thought and education at New York University.

He served as consulting expert in education to the United States Holocaust Memorial Council.

He is also an active member of the Coalition for the Advancement of Jewish Education and was chairperson of the International CAJE Conference in Jerusalem.

Mr. Rossel, his wife Karen, and their twin daughters Amy and Deborah live along Golden Creek in Dallas, Texas.